Playing Better Soccer
Is More Fun

By Larry Paul

West Chicago Public Library District
118 West Washington
West Chicago, IL 60185-2803
Phone # (630) 231-1552

A Comprehensive Guide to the

Small-Sided Games Coaching Model

Published by Accotink Press

5444 Calvin Court, Springfield, VA 22151

Printed by Signature Book Printing

www.sbpbooks.com

ISBN: 1 – 932433 – 58 – 9

Library of Congress Cataloging Control Number

2005911094

Project Editor: Kate Achelpohl

Design © Accotink Press, 2005

Copyright © Larry Paul 2005

TXu 1 – 250 – 676

Accotink

Press

About the Author

Larry Paul has been involved in soccer at all levels for over thirty years. As a founding member of the Washington Area Girls Soccer League, author of the Internationally respected coaching resource, *www.bettersoccermorefun.com*, the *DVD Street Soccer, An Introduction to Small-Sided Games* as well as several articles in the N.S.C.A.A.'s *Soccer Journal* he has been in the forefront of youth soccer education. He holds the U.S.S.F. A License, The Football Associations International Preliminary Badge and the K.N.V.B.'s Introductory Coaching Certificate. He is currently the Program Director for the Chris Nedelcovych Soccer Foundation, a member of the Maryland State Youth Soccer Associations Education and Training Department and the Technical Director for the Burke Athletic Club.

Playing Better Soccer Is More Fun

A portion of the proceeds from the sale of this book will be donated to the Chris Nedelcovych Soccer Foundation, a registered 501-c-3 non-profit organization dedicated to the mission of promoting "Youth Coaching Youth." For more information on the CNSF visit *www.cnsfund.org.*

For Becky, without whose support this book
would not have been possible.

Foreword

"My idea when I was a player was that when the team was good, it couldn't go badly for me. Training Too. When the team played good football, you enjoy the people. And you never know in advance if you're going to become champions. All you can do is play good football. That's why, when you see 50 matches, you watch with pleasure 40 times. 40 good days; that's what you work for."

Johan Cruyff, - <u>Ajax, Barcelona, Cruyff, The ABC of an Obstinate Maestro</u>
Frits Barend and Henk van Dorp, 1997 Bloomsbury

Several years ago I started conducting State Level Coaching Courses for the Maryland State Youth Soccer Association. I was fortunate to be working with very experienced people in an excellent program. I was familiar with the content, comfortable with making the presentations and ready to go out and spread the gospel.

One of the challenges that I faced was bringing value to coaches from diverse backgrounds. There were parent coaches who had been involved with the game for only a few months, former Youth National Pool players and some old North American Soccer League veterans. I had to keep everyone engaged while not leaving anyone behind. Information had to be fresh and practical.

My presentation began to draw, more and more, from my experience with small-sided games. Combined with a covert teaching style they proved to be effective and enjoyable for everyone involved. It was a return to the old street soccer days. I saw this as a way to keep the experienced coaches from becoming bored while giving the new coaches something they could successfully do, organize the session and let the games do the heavy lifting.

This book is based on my experience from those courses along with many years of practical coaching. You can start at the beginning and treat it as a self-contained course, or skip straight to the games and go right to work. Either way, whether you're brand new to the sport or an old hand at the game you're bound to find more then a few new ideas here.

Good luck and good soccer.

Larry Paul

Table of Contents

Chapter 1

Who, Me Coach?!

Shh! Listen! Did you hear that? It's the lament of the new coaches, a biennial cry by tens of thousands of presumably competent adults across America: "I can't coach soccer! I don't know anything about coaching!"

It's not altogether true, and even if it was, it's too late. You're the coach — maybe because you checked "yes" next to that volunteer question on your kids' registration form, or because you answered the phone when the league director called and said woefully, "If you don't take on the coach's responsibility, there won't be a team — and (sigh) none of the children will be able to play." Regardless, it's a done deal.

Even if you don't know how to inflate a soccer ball, odds are you have at least some idea of what a coach is supposed to do, thanks to movies and television: Remember Craig T. Nelson, in "Coach" and Billy Bob Thornton in "Friday Night Lights"? And you must have learned something from your weekly overdose of sports news. In any case, it's the rare adult that takes the field without some type of model in mind.

So before you meet the kids for practice, you get the administrative jobs out of the way: set up telephone trees, attend a coaches' meeting, obtain a field permit, find a few soccer balls and cones, organize the half time snack rotation, speak with every parent, help organize car pools and review the schedule. Once all that's accomplished, the easy part is over and the work begins.

In this book we'll look at how to coach soccer and give even the least-experienced coaches a clear, step-by-step guide for practices and games. And never fear, soccer vets, there's a few new ideas for you old timers too.

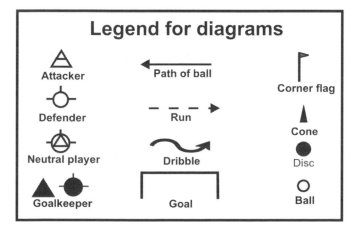

Send the PE Teacher Back to School

Forget the movies or TV the most common model for coaching is the physical education teacher. Soccer is physical! Coaching involves education! Sounds like a perfect fit. Get some cones, a whistle and a clipboard. Put the kids in organized lines while they patiently wait to take their turn running drills; teach them the rules and basic strategy. Throw in some stretches to avoid injury, a short jog for cardio vascular fitness and ta-da! it's a practice. It's controlled and methodical — and appears to cover every base!

Unfortunately, the P.E. coaching model doesn't work very well for competitive team sports. It's great for controlling students and evaluating isolated techniques and knowledge. But those techniques and knowledge are usually removed from the actual game; students in phys ed class are rarely evaluated based on their performance in a competitive match.

Of course it's important to learn how to pass the ball back and forth, but the learning must go deeper. For instance, what if the other team has the ball and won't share? Small-sided games will bridge the gap between the structure of the P.E. class and soccer's competitive, chaotic nature. They allow you to coach while giving the children the opportunity to learn within the context of an actual game.

On the surface, you and the kids' P.E. teachers have the same job — to introduce students/players to the game and help them master fundamentals. However, while the P.E. teacher's objective is to prepare the students for a skills test at the end of their soccer unit, yours is to prepare them to compete.

Remember, Coach: Your players are looking for ways to win, not grades. Their "evaluation," as individuals and as a team, is based on their performance in a real game against real opponents. The fluid, chaotic setting of soccer resembles recess more than P.E. class. Learning in this environment will require a different model.

The Physical Education model is designed around the teacher/coach maintaining control through the use of lines, laps and lectures. The teacher/coach is the main source of information and is directly responsible for "teaching."

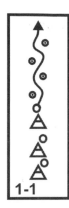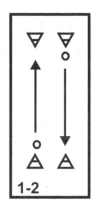 Diagrams 1-1 and 1-2 show typical drills physical education teachers use to teach and evaluate dribbling and passing. In 1-1, the students line up and take turns dribbling through a series of cones. In 1-2, two students stand across from each other and pass a ball back and forth. The teacher observes the students actions and assigns them a grade based on their technical proficiency.

Soccer players, on the other hand, play in a world marked by a chaotic and rapidly changing environment. They never get the opportunity to take a turn without active opposition. Their objective for each individual action, and ultimately the game varies, but is always based on whether or not they were succesful. They're graded based of the result and not on the effort. It's a completely different goal from Physical Education.

No Lines, No Laps, No Lectures

United States Youth Soccer (www.usyouthsoccer.org) is a non-profit educational organization whose mission is to foster the physical, mental and emotional growth and development of America's youth through the sport of soccer at all ages and competitive levels, to make soccer fun and instill a lifelong passion for the sport. They provide the guiding principles for soccer education in the United States.

The small-sided games model of coaching follows the U.S. Youth Soccer's mantra, "no lines, no laps, no lectures," encouraging the children to learn by playing small-sided games, e.g., 2v2, 3v3 up to 8v8. This way you'll effectively eliminate the primary tools of the P.E. model. The small-sided games model requires you to construct simplified forms of soccer each one centering on a real soccer problem. The children learn how to play the game by mastering each simplified form.

Your job in this model is to help the players play better in each of the forms. In effect, to help them play a simplified form of soccer better. It really is that simple. Everything you do as a coach contributes to this single objective: Players with better technique play better soccer. Fitter players have more stamina and play better soccer. Advanced concepts make them smarter (i.e., better) players. Everything a coach does is driven by the end goal of helping the players play the game at a higher level, now and in the future. And there is a simplified form to meet almost every need.

> **The small-sided games model is designed around the players solving simplified soccer problems with their skills. The game is the main source of instruction and the focus is on learning as opposed to teaching.**

Soccer is a Game – Play On

But before we can help the children play better soccer, we need to understand what soccer is. In its broadest sense soccer is simply a game that occupies leisure time. It's a hobby so we'll start with that.

Chances are good that none of the children on your team is currently making a career out of playing soccer. Children, like adults, often try something new. It might just be a fad and or it may grow into a passion. In any case, people approach their hobbies differently then they approach work or school. The time and effort invested is voluntary, and they respond to direction and instruction in a different way than they do as students or employees. They can take it or leave it and usually want to have some input in the process themselves. One of the first things that your players learn is how much effort they want to invest in the game and whether the returns justify the investment.

Games revolve around solving problems; the more difficult the problem, the harder the game. Soccer requires solving soccer problems, and it's a hard game to master. Like a harmonica, it's easy to play, but difficult to play well. It requires a high level of skill, and the fact that opponents can interfere makes it even harder.

The games end in a result, which provides feedback. Whether it's an individual dual or the final result of the match when you win, you solved the problem. When you lose, you didn't. It's that simple. Because this type of feedback is immediate and independent of any external source like a coach or a parent, it frees you up to do your job. You don't have to tell the kids how they did, they already know. It also helps children learn to evaluate themselves, using the result as a measure and developing their own internalized value structure.

Now we'll look at what makes soccer different from any other game.

Team Play Requires Teamwork

Soccer is a game of us vs. them. It requires cooperation (with teammates) and competition (opponents) simultaneously. We have to solve the problems that they give us and give them problems that they can't solve, all in the same moment. Learning how to juggle these demands, to work together and to help others play better is an important step in player development. It means that children are beginning to consider the game and the team from outside their own perspective.

But competition puts cooperation to the test. You learn more about the children's character when things are going wrong then when they are going right. That's when fingers start pointing and some players try to solve all the problems themselves while others simply shut down. In other words, human nature comes into play.

Successfully working through these issues is every bit as important as successfully completing a wall pass, and learning how to deal with tension is part of a player's development. Later on, we'll cover how to use and control the level of tension in small-sided games. It's is an important coaching skill.

Goals – Direction and Objectives

In soccer the objective is to score goals while preventing the opponent from scoring. Scoring, not scoring, being scored on or stopping a goal activates a feedback loop, one that tells the players how well they are doing. So goals give the game meaning.

When the goals are at opposite ends of the field they give the game direction — e.g., up and back, north and south — and supply a center. Left and right keep their point of reference, so players have at least a geographic fix on the field. Without goals opposite each other the game lacks this element.

The field – Boundaries

The field sets the limits for what is in and out of play.

Using space, an important concept and skill in soccer, starts with understanding its limits — there's only so much usable space available. In the beginning children learn that there are boundaries and that crossing them has consequences. For example, playing the ball off the field means that the other team will get it. It's another example of a feedback loop.

The Ball – Possession Determines Role

You play soccer with a ball, have you every tried playing without one? No-Touch soccer! It's a Zen kinda thing! The ball is a critical element, yet it is amazing how much soccer training is done without one.

Rules – Sets Limits and Controls Behavior

Lots of games have two teams competing against each other. Many games are played on a field. Many even have goals on opposite ends of the field and quite a few use a ball. While the goals and the field have already supplied two basic, important rules (how we'll score and where the game takes place), it's the rest of the rules that make each game unique. Soccer has soccer rules. You need rules to start and restart the game, to set limits and control behavior. By controlling the rules along with the field and goals you can define what techniques and skills will be necessary in order to play the game properly.

> **Soccer is a game made up of specific elements. It's played by two teams and has a goal at each end of a defined field. Each team scores in one goal and defends the other. The game has soccer rules and uses a ball.**

These elements define what soccer is. We'll look at each one in greater detail in Chapters Two and Three.

While all of this might seem obvious, a quick trip to many practice fields reveals children working on something other then soccer. Activities that lack goals, opponents, even a ball keep children busy and are often mistaken for the game. They can have the appearance of soccer activities but they aren't, they are something else.

Drills like dribbling through cones or passing a ball back and forth, the P.E. examples above, lack a significant number of soccer elements. Time spent in these types of activities is generally lost. Players don't become bored, they begin bored and it goes downhill from there. While these activities may have a place in the educational system, they are an inefficient use of time for the majority of parent coaches.

By using and manipulating the elements of soccer, small-sided games provide the most natural, efficient and effective way for children to learn the game. Not only can they learn all of the techniques and tactics in these forms they are free to find their own solutions to problems, an important part in developing creativity. They are just as free to determine their own level of involvement, an important part in developing responsibility.

Chapter 2

Play with the Elements

As we saw in Chapter 1 soccer is made up of certain, readily identifiable elements. Learning how to use them to create and manage small-sided games will take some time and practice and is an essential skill in the small-sided games model. This chapter will look at each element in greater detail and provide you with insight on some variations.

The Game

The first step in coaching with small-sided games is to identify the problem that you want to address. Then you need to decide how difficult the problem should be for the players.

Creating your practice game is a bit like conducting a scientific experiment. You adjust the variables, the elements, one at a time and hold the other's constant. If they aren't mixed to create the problem at the level you want, the game won't do its job. So first, first adjust the game, than coach the players.

Build each game around an actual soccer problem your team faces. For example, we'll say John, a back player, is one of your slower players. Were you his track coach, you might look at the problem as "John doesn't run fast enough." But as his soccer coach, you need to frame the issue in terms of its effects on his soccer playing — e.g., "John gets to the ball too late when opponents play the deep pass."

More often than not you'll need more than one session to solve any given problem. Part of your job at each practice is to choose which game you'll use, decide how long to use it and how hard it should be. Keep an eye on how each player is handling the game. You may have to adjust it — up or down — several times before you find the correct mix. Tweak the elements until it's just right. Changes in the teams, the goals, the field, the rules and even the characteristics of the ball can all make the game easier or harder. And remember, sometimes your players simply won't have what it takes to duplicate the level they played at during the last practice. You might need to lower the level of the game in order to meet your objectives for the practice.

Once you're able to create the problem at the right level of difficulty, you need to make sure it repeats — a lot. There's little point in playing a game for 10 minutes and only seeing the problem once or twice. The "coachable moments" need to happen repeatedly so the players cannot deny the problem and are forced to solve it. You want it to keep coming back to haunt them. However, too much trouble, e.g. resistance, isn't good either. Strike a balance so your players can see the light at the end of the tunnel as they practice their solutions.

Earlier we discussed how results provide feedback for the players, which helps to shape and drive their internal motivation. Each player has to care about the quality and the final product of the team's effort. Children need to learn how to support each other when the result goes against them, and how to offer and receive constructive criticism. The best teachers in this effort are their teammates. With the small-sided games model, you'll create a team of mini-coaches!

By incorporating a lot of small-sided games in training, you include the experience of winning and losing. Children get to fill their "won-lost bank accounts" with the currency of understanding the transient nature of results. After a while, the highs and lows of winning and losing level off. This is a big step in developing the correct mentality needed for the next level of play and helps them to lower their fear of failure.

Teams

Since a change in the number of players can have such a dramatic impact on the lesson we'll devote the next chapter to this subject. Here we'll look at one factor in the teams that has more to do with the rules then the numbers, the goalkeeper.

Playing With or Without Goalkeepers

The goalkeeper's position is unique; they are the only player allowed to use their hands on the field. When you use them in small-sided games it influences the rest of the players and the nature of the game itself.

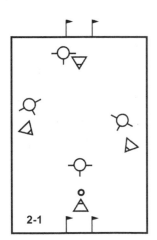

Diagram 2-1 shows a basic 4v4 situation with the sweeper bringing the ball out. Each player has an immediate opponent and the game is essentially based on man-to-man action. Every player has a clear task and it's only a question of execution as to which team will prevail.

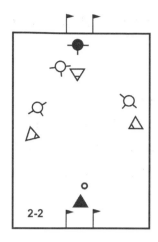

In Diagram 2-2, each team has replaced one of their field players with a goalkeeper. The 4v4 game becomes 3v3 with goalkeepers.

This situation still leaves the three defenders with man-to-man responsibilities, the same as in Diagram 2-1. But if the goalkeeper in possession brings the ball out, he or she becomes a free attacker. Their "immediate opponent" is the opposing goalkeeper. In this case, the three field defenders face the dilemma of deciding who goes to the attacking goalkeeper, leaving their own player open. By acting proactively the attackers can create a numbers up situation — 2v1, 3v2 or 4v3 — that the defenders will have to deal with.

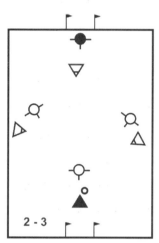

Diagram 2-3 shows one solution to the problem: The defenders elect to mark the goalkeeper. This prevents him or her from bringing the ball out, but leaves another attacker open on the field. A throw from the goalkeeper to the open top player will take the three defenders out of the game and leaves a 1vGK situation in front of the goal. This is not a good solution for the defenders.

Note: Defenders only need to mark the goalkeeper if he or she fills their attacking role like a field player and goes forward when they are unopposed, Diagram 2-2. This forces the defenders to respond to the immediate threat posed by the player with the ball. It's a moot point if the goalkeeper doesn't take this responsibility as well as a rigid interpretation of the player's tasks. A goalkeeper in possession is an attacker first, and a goalkeeper second. We'll cover these tasks in greater detail in Chapter 4.

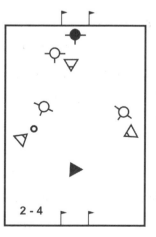

Diagram 2-4 shows how goalkeepers can limit a team's mobility, one of the principles of play. If this was simply a game of 4v4, the sweeper (the dark triangle/goalkeeper), might consider moving past the player with the ball. One of the midfielders would temporarily take over his or her role, and the defending team would face a new problem. But in this case the last player is a goalkeeper, and since only goalkeepers may use their hands a midfielder cannot fully take on their role. This puts a damper on everyone and limits the offensive options for both teams. In this case, while the goalkeeper is an attacker, their practical use will be limited. (The old street soccer rule, last man back is the goalkeeper takes this into account. It allows you to use goalkeepers without limiting the teams attacking potential.)

So including goalkeepers in the game can change the picture you're looking at, the plan the players need to follow and the options they have available to them.

Goals Provide Direction, Objectives and Feedback

Goals — the physical landmarks — are an essential part of the feedback mechanism necessary for learning. Your teams will want to know which way to go and how to score. The clearest answer comes with big goals, nets and a live goalkeeper. But this isn't always possible, or even desirable, at practice. When you're tweaking your small-sided games, keep this in mind — and consider some options.

Basic Goals, Basic Game

The basic game uses two goals of the same size opposite each other. This is the most realistic way to play and the form where you always start with or return to.

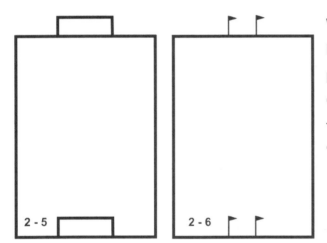

Whether you're using real goals, Diagram 2-5, corner flags, Diagram 2-6 or a just a couple of cones the basic game presents a level playing field with a clear objective. Children can learn the meaning of all four directions — forward, backwards, right, left — as well as "inside," "outside" and "center" within the context of the game.

Adjust the Size of the Goals

Changing the size of the goals can have a dramatic effect on the game. Larger goals are harder to defend, which can result in more scoring. To counter this, teams must adapt their style of play using guidelines like: Play in the opponent's half; when in possession keep the ball; apply immediate pressure when you lose the ball; try to win the ball back as far from your goal as possible and more players will have a defensive role in the basic plan.

With larger goals comes a greater degree of tension. The consequences of a mistake are magnified by the swift feedback of the opponent's response, a goal conceded. (Playing with big goals and without goalkeepers can increase this.) One benefit: Games like this help players learn how to maintain their concentration and improve their overall defensive qualities. It's a good way to develop the defensive skills in 1v1.

Shrinking the goal size has the opposite effect. Small targets require fewer defenders, who can afford to defend nearer to the goal. And because a single person can block the direct route to the goal, it's not so crucial to place immediate pressure on the opponents when you lose possession. Likewise, with less tension and less at stake the recovery run becomes the recovery jog.

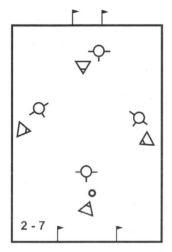

In Diagram 2-7, the goal at the top is small enough that one person can block it with very little help; if the opponents don't score within seconds of winning the ball they may never score at all. The goal at the bottom is so large that two players could not adequately defend it by standing on the line. The only option is to keep the opponents as far away from the goal as possible and to defend with a large number of players. That can take a lot of energy and isn't much fun, so players soon learn to avoid defending by not giving the ball away when they have it.

Create a Dead Zone with Recessed Goals

Changing the size of the goals can create problems that you don't want. Large goals and poor defending may not challenge the attackers. Small goals can be clogged by a single defender — the worst player on the team can stifle and frustrate even the best players by simply occupying the scoring space.

One remedy to these situations is to place the goals from 2-10 yards off the field. This creates a recessed goal with a dead zone between the field and the goals. Now the defender cannot stand in the goal and is, in effect, forced to play out from it. The defender who stays on the goal line is still some distance from the goal, and that gives attackers plenty of room to shoot around them.

There are other benefits to using recessed goals. They eliminate the short tap or dribble in goals. Even the 5- and 6-year olds will have to 'shoot' at least 2 or 3 yards to score. When the goals are 8 or 10 yards off of the field, players have to get their heads up to look for the deep pass. Since they'll usually be shooting from inside the field, they will be trying to hit a target 12 to 18 yards away. Young players are limited in their 'sphere of consciousness' and moving the goals off of the field will help them to expand the area of which they're aware. (This works especially well when combined with the rule that you can only score with a shot on the ground. In this case players are practicing finding and making the deep pass.)

Finally, the dead zone creates a safe haven for young goalkeepers. By putting the goals 3-4 yards off of the field they will only have to deal with shot stopping and distribution. They won't have to worry about being confronted with a mob situation or attackers coming in uncontested. The space immediately in front and around them will be free of distractions.

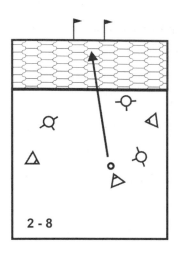

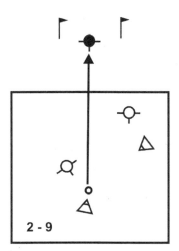

Diagram 2-8 shows the attacker shooting from inside the field with the goal a few yards removed. Shooting the ball over a long distance takes considerably more and quicker skill. In the time that the attacking player will need to shoot, the defender can close in to block or even tackle the ball. Players who overestimate their abilities will get a quick lesson, i.e., feedback, when their shots get blocked or don't even reach the goal. For the defenders they'll feel less compelled to drop back and "defend the goal." For younger players recessed goals can be more conducive to man-to-man marking, which encourages 1v1.

Diagram 2-9 shows how recessed goals can be used to effectively create a goalkeeper's safe zone. Without having a lot of players immediately around them, even novice goalkeepers will find it easier to track the ball and become familiar with distance, angles and handling the ball. It also offers them the free space to practice restarting the game with a player's choice. In this example the goalkeeper could put the ball down and bring it on the field themselves. This would create a numbers up situation for the goalkeeper's team. (The sweeper-keeper game, described in Chapter 11, uses this situation to teach when to build up and when to counterattack.)

Multiple Goal Games

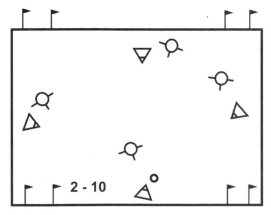

The placement of the goals in the basic game creates a situation where both teams finish their attacks in the center of the field. This is realistic, after all that's where you score in real soccer. However, by placing two or more small goals on the goal line as shown in Diagram 2-10, your game maintains the element of direction, but you create a situation where the teams can score on a much wider front. (The four-goal game shown in Diagram 2-10 is described in detail in Chapter 11.)

Line Soccer

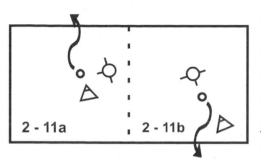

2 - 11a   2 - 11b

Line soccer, like the four-goal game, encourages attacking along a broad front, because the entire end line is a goal. But, rather than shoot the ball into a goal, players score by dribbling the ball across the line, Diagrams 2-11a&b. The dribble must be under control, not just a kick and run. You can add a shallow channel in which to stop the ball or even stop the ball on the line itself to score. When you take shooting out of the picture, teams have to use the whole field to score.

Line soccer is one of the most underutilized goals in the coach's tool kit. It changes the game dramatically and encourages players to try their talent in 1v1. Just like in a player's choice restart, your coaching will largely center on helping them to recognize the correct moment when to make their move.

Use a Target as a "Goal"

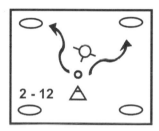

2 - 12

Scoring a goal in line soccer requires dribbling the ball across the line, usually with some speed, often pursued by a defender. Using a target such as a hoop, Diagram 2-12, or simply stopping the ball within a yard of the corner, requires the dribbler to come to a stop in a limited space to score. They cannot over run their target so they'll have to beat their opponent convincingly.

Targets, like line soccer retain the game's direction. There is a goal in front to attack and one behind to defend. The difference between these games and the basic game is in what skills are being emphasized. In small versions of line soccer and targets, i.e. 2v2 and 3v3, both sides of 1v1 will come into play. In the basic game you could play for 10 minutes, never have a 1v1, and still make a significant contribution to the team. The different types of goals place different demands on the players.

End Zone Games Keep Up the Pace

An end zone is a defined area at each end of the field that can be used as a goal, Diagram 2-13. For example your game may require a team to play line soccer into the end zone or to pass the ball to a teammate who is already inside it. You can condition the later game by requiring that the ball cross into the end zone before the receiver, duplicating a through pass into space for the player to run onto.

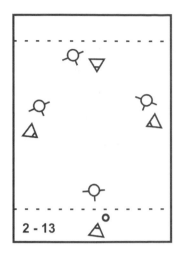

End zone games can run north-south and then south-north. After a team scores they don't have to return to their end of the field. Instead, they can keep the ball and try to score again, going in the opposite direction. This saves time, and the 'winners' of each point get the benefit of continuing on the attack. Plus, the defenders have some extra motivation to stop their opponents— they want the attacking role and they can't have it until they win the ball. Changing the direction of the attack is just like switching sides at half time; it doesn't eliminate the direction of the game. Each team still has a goal in front to attack and one behind to defend, no matter which end zone they start from.

Use Neutral Players for Goals

When neutral players, discussed in Chapter 3, serve as goals it adds the element of uneven numbers. For example, adding a neutral player to each end of the field, Diagram 2-14, makes the 3v3 game 5v3. (5 is the team in possession.) In a simple version of this game, one neutral player starts it by playing the ball to one of the teams. That team scores by getting the ball to the other neutral player. They repeat the process, going north-south and then south-north, until the other team wins the ball, passes it to a neutral player and starts the process themselves.

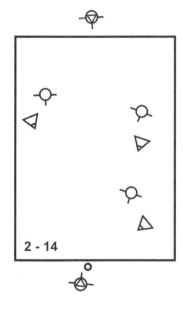

When the ball goes out of play, a designated neutral player restarts the game by playing a new ball into the team that has possession. The neutral players can move anywhere along the end line, or you can limit this area, to receive a pass. You can also put restrictions on the neutral players — for example, one/two touch, don't let the ball stop or don't pass the ball back to the player who gave it to them. You can add a very shallow end zone for the neutral players and the rule that any pass that leaves the end zone means a change in possession. This will require the field players to be very accurate passing to the neutral players. Nothing wide, or through, the target will work. You and an assistant can get a lot of use out of this game by participating as the neutral players. You can keep the game moving at a very fast pace which keeps the players concentrating. This makes it a good game for working on the mentality and skills needed in building up the attack.

Combine Objectives

Goals represent objectives. When both teams have the same objective, use the same goal. But there are two situations where you can benefit from having the teams use different goals. The first is when you need to equalize an imbalance between the teams; for example, you can make the better team's goal larger, or give them an extra goal to defend, because the handicap will create a more level playing field.

The other situation is where the teams have different objectives. For example, if one team needs to practice building up out of the back, have it attack small goals or play line soccer. Because their opponents will be trying to stop them, they will attack a full size goal with a goalkeeper. In order for the feedback to be relevant the goals have to reflect the objective of the team.

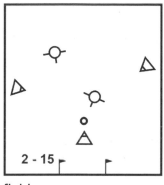

The game illustrated in Diagram 2-15 uses combined goals to even the disparity in the numbers. The three attackers score by playing line soccer, while the two defenders score in the small goal. The triangles must combine to carry the ball the full length of the field. If one of them stays back to protect the goal the numbers game changes from 3v2 to 2v2. If all three attackers come forward they have the advantage of being a man up, but risk the possibility that if they make a mistake the defenders will punish them with a quick shot from anywhere on the field.

Objectives as "Goals"

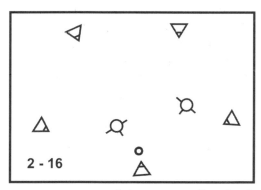

An objective can also serve as a "goal." A good example is 5v2, Diagram 2-16, a possession game in which a five player-team tries to complete a certain number of passes (we'll cover this game in Chapter 11). When they do, they've scored. But when objectives are used the game will lack physical direction. It can flow any way, which makes pressurizing extremely difficult, and ideas like goal side, blind side or off sides irrelevant. While objective-based games can serve a useful purpose, they're less realistic than other game models. They resemble coach's games and not player's games.

Specialty Goals for Specific Problems

Specialty goals have the same problem as objectives. They too can be very useful for addressing a specific issue, especially a particular technique. But there are so many elements missing that these games can fall short of being 'real soccer.' For example, soccer tennis, while it teaches children how to deal with the ball in the air, an important technical concern, it certainly wouldn't be confused with a soccer match. We'll look at how objectives and specialty goals can be used effectively in the Chapter 11.

Play with the Field: Adjust it to Your Needs

The field represents the usable playing area. In a match the dimensions and layout are set but in training you have the flexibility to adjust it to fit your own needs.

Whenever you set up a game, take the first few minutes and simply observe what is going on. Does the size of the field suit what you want? Do the players have enough or too much space? You need to apply the Goldilocks rule — this field is too big; this field is too small; this field is just right — because it's only on a "just right" field that the game is going to work. The dimensions that you get out of any book, including this one, are only guidelines and you need to adjust them to fit your own situation. Consider some factors that can affect the size of the field:

- **The number of players:** Changing the numbers in a game can directly impact the space the players need. When you add or take players out of a game, watch for a few minutes to see how the change has affected the play.

- **The soccer ages and abilities of the players:** Generally speaking, more talented players need less space, so don't be surprised if a team of talented 10-year-olds needs less room than beginning 12-year-olds.

- **The condition of the field:** Fast fields, those without grass or ones that are rock hard, result in faster ball speed and players will need more space to react. Slow fields are the worst situation, especially when there's high grass, which makes dribbling and passes on the ground difficult at best. In this case the players often resort to lofting the ball and you may need to compensate for that. Grass clumps, divots and ruts can cause bad bounces, so if the field has a lot of them, you may need extra space.

- **The needs of the game:** The dimensions can vary from game to game. For example, a counterattacking game needs a very long, but narrow, field. It can be played in areas that you wouldn't even consider playing the basic game.

- **Channels and zones:** There will be times, such as when you use end zones as goals, when you will want to 'subdivide' your field. The breakout games in Chapter 11 are also good examples of this.

Play with the Rules

Changing the rules that apply on the field during the game is the simplest way to influence the training — you don't even need to set up any equipment!

Rules to Start and Restart Play

The most important rule in small-sided games is how the game will start and restart. Each game is built around a specific lesson, and by presenting it at every restart, you'll ensure the sheer quantity of repetition you need. So the start/restarting point of the game should lead very quickly, if not directly, to the learning point.

There are literally hundreds of small-sided games used for training. But all of those games can be grouped into two categories — free-form and reload games — depending on the restart rules.

The free-form game, which places no restrictions on the players' positions when the game is restarted, is most common. The restart itself might be restricted, but the players are free to move wherever they see fit. You just get the game going.

The major advantage of free form games is that the kids can really build up a head of steam. Games can be played for long periods at a fairly high level, duplicating the ups and downs of the pace in real games. One minute the game is fast; the next it slows down. Also, once they get going, players usually don't require much monitoring, and that can free you up to step back and observe. Finally, they are just plain fun. Basic free form games are the closest thing to playing soccer — which is why the children have come to practice in the first place.

In training, the idea usually is to simply to get the game going again, and free form games can include any or all of the traditional restarts. But don't sweat the small stuff: Too great an emphasis on the "real rules" can get in the way of the fun and objectives of the practice. For example, having 6-year-olds take throw-ins and corners can bring the game to a stop.

Below are some other options for a practice restart:

- **Player's Choice:** The player with the ball will decide whether to dribble or pass the ball in, it's their choice. Once the ball has re-entered the field, the game is live and that player will have to live with the consequences of their decision. This is a first class choice because with every restart the player with the ball has to decide "Do I pass or do I dribble?"

- **First Pass Free:** This is a good way to restart possession games like 5v2. Restart the ball from on or off the field, but the defenders cannot block the pass or move until the receiver of the first pass has touched the ball. The game begins at that moment.

- **New Ball In:** The game does not have to resume with the same ball that went out. As soon as the ball goes out of play, a new ball gets passed (by a member of the team in possession, a neutral player or a coach) to the team that has possession. This rule eliminates retrieval time. When players get used to this restart the games can become very intense and focused. There is very little time to relax and lose concentration. While the new ball does not need to enter the field where the old one went out your players will need to know who will play the new ball in, where they will be, and when to expect the new ball.

- **Free Ball In:** This is a lot like "new ball in," but there's a twist. While players know who will put the new ball in and where they are after one goes out of play, there's no guarantee which team will get possession. It's best if you handle this restart yourself — and have an agenda. For example, watch for opportunities to set up an easy situation in the game for a player who lacks confidence dribbling or look for two players and put the ball where they'll have to battle for it. You'll be able to pick the right moment and situation to achieve your coaching objective.

- **Slam Ball Restart:** This restart involves slamming the ball on the ground so that there is an element of uncertainty in who will get possession. The sound of the ball hitting the ground signals the start, but with it drifting up and floating down the players have a few seconds to read the situation.

In a reload game players must return to set positions before every restart. This slows the game down, breaking up the flow and wasting valuable time while the players get back to their "reload positions." However, the biggest benefit is that every restart can lead directly into the learning moment and this can make up for the lost time.

When you control where the players are and the method to start the game, everybody knows what to expect, and the game usually goes from "0 to 60" in two seconds. The pace is hard to maintain, so most reload games have a very short life, a matter of a few, (10 to 30) seconds. Then the players have to return to the starting positions and do it again. The constant reloading makes these games feel like a coaches' game. (Players would never come up with these games on their own!) Reload games are valuable to prove a point, but quickly get old.

Rules as Limiting Factors

Placing a condition on the game is one of the oldest tricks in the training book. A limitation such as two-touch (to force additional passing) will apply to both teams and can be a good way to work on basic problems. The rule becomes a central feature of the lesson and requires both teams to play in a predictable way.

However, here's a warning for you: Conditions create artificial situations, and if over-used, they can teach bad habits. If, for example, you only have them playing two-touch, your players might develop a fantastic passing game but would have no idea how to win a 1v1 duel. Use conditions sparingly, for a specific purpose, for short periods and always balanced with the 'other side of the coin.'

A few common conditions are:

- **One touch:** Only the best players are capable of playing this with close or even teams. The requirements on the individual TIC are very high, and the speed of the game can quickly get out of control. It is a useful rule when applied to neutral players or large uneven numbers like 5v2. (See Chapter 9 for an explanation of TIC.)

- **Two touch:** A slower game than one touch, even talented 10 year olds can play it. Children get the opportunity to control the ball, look over the field and make their pass. They still have the option to play the ball first time.

- **Three or fewer touches:** This rule allows players to go on mini-dribbles, with one touch to control the ball, one to beat an opponent and one to pass. Talented players can do a lot within these limits.

- **Must use three or more touches:** Players can touch the ball as many times as they like, as long as it's at least three times. This slows the game down considerably, forcing everyone to do a little dribbling. It eliminates 'one touch boot ball,' gets players into trouble that they'll have to work their own way out of and offers lots of opportunities to tackle.

- **Ball can't stop:** The team in possession must keep the ball moving which limits the amount of time players have to think and act. (If the ball does stop, the opponents get an indirect kick where it did.) Add a touch restriction, and the players will be forced to think ahead so they have their passing options in mind before they receive the ball. Otherwise, they'll only have a few seconds to make a decision. The speed of play will increase considerably.

- **One touch to score:** Limiting shooting to one touch and you duplicate a common situation — 60 percent of all goals are scored with only one touch — and force players to quickly decide whether to shoot or pass. Players soon learn how to lurk and pick up the garbage goals. This rule works best in games of 4v4 or larger.

- **A set number of passes before scoring:** Establish how many passes a team must make before they can score. This rule places a strong emphasis on how well a team builds its attack and keeps possession of the ball at the expense of the quick counterattack.

- **Keep the ball below the knees or on the ground:** The best way to move the ball is on the ground, yet many youth teams have the ball up in the air so much their games resemble a NASA experiment gone awry. Forcing children to keep the ball down makes it easier for their teammates to receive the pass and is a key step in improving speed of play.

- **Score from the air only:** Goals can only be scored when the scorer receives the ball in the air and before it touches the ground. Use some big goals, a couple of neutral players and after awhile you'll see bicycle kicks, side volleys, players juggling for shots and headers. And the other side of the coin, defending in the air, will be emphasized as well.

- **No returning the ball to the player who gave it to you:** The ball tends to have a hypnotic effect on children. As a result, they too often give the ball back to the player who just passed to them; a series of give-and-goes with individual dribbles in between. This rule forces the kids to break that pattern, pushing them to find a 'third attacker' and helping to open up the field. And because two or three other attackers must become an option after every pass, the rule helps everyone else keep concentrating. (This rule effectively takes one attacker off of the field, so a neutral player might help to keep the teams even.)

- **Offsides:** This is a good rule to use when you want to make the game harder for the attackers. It encourages the back players to push up quickly and play as a unit. It forces a higher level of communication and tension between the players. You can even play without goalkeepers by assuming that he or she is on the field and only counting the offsides when the attacker gets behind the last field player.

Equalizing Rules Level the Playing Field

Establish a rule, such as any of the ones above, and apply it to only one team to equalize a disparity (e.g., a superstar who dominates the game). This can also be useful when your team is running away with a match. By putting a restriction on your players they can continue learning even when the opponents can't provide any reasonable resistance.

Changing a rule is a simple way to have a profound effect on the game. It allows you to focus on a new problem or to quickly get a game under control by changing the level of resistance. Just keep in mind the KISS principle: Keep it short and simple. Only use rules that help the game. Too many, or overly complicated ones, can confuse the players, lower the level of enjoyment and defeat your purpose.

Create Consequences

Consequence rules are designed to reinforce and add significance to the lesson by giving players something more than bragging rights to shoot for.

- **Winner stays:** Set up three teams. Two play a short game, and the winner stays on the field to play the third team. Repeat as often as you like — although you can limit the number of games one team may play at a time. If there aren't enough players to make three full teams, then the losing team can choose a player(s) to stay on and play. (Use a traditional method, such as "Rock, Paper, Scissors" to choose who stays on and joins the new team.) Winner Stays helps children understand and build a healthy respect for the difference between winning and losing. The consequences are immediate and easy to understand: If you win, you keep playing. If you lose, you don't.

- **Knock out:** Some games, like four square, are built on the idea of putting someone out. The idea is to stay in the game as long as possible even at someone else's expense. It's Winner Stays rule, but on an individual level.

- **Give away, go away:** Reinforce the importance of ball possession. The player who loses the ball* — by either playing it out of bounds, losing it in a tackle or giving up an interception — temporarily leaves the field to run around a goal or a point outside of midfield while play continues. There are dual consequences here: Temporarily leaving the game means that the player's team will have to play one person down until their teammate returns to the field, so the team suffers just as much as the individual. (And the player's teammates are likely to speak their minds about that!) It also makes players think about who's at fault — the passer or the receiver? — when a pass is intercepted. This thought process opens the children to start talking to each other about the details of the game, because they begin to see that they all have a vested interest in them.

*To avoid discouraging attacking play, exempt goal kicks from the rule, and/or divide the field into 'attacking zones,' in which the rule doesn't apply.

- **Tournaments:** Small, fast 2v2 or 3v3 tournaments are a good way to start a practice. You can play as a mini-league or a knock-out cup competition with the winners getting the universally appreciated "Great Job!"

- **Three Corners is a Goal:** When corner kicks are not used in small-sided games, clever players quickly figure out how to use this to their advantage. Whenever they get into trouble, they give away what should be a corner, and get to restart the game with a goal kick. While you have to give them credit for solving the problem, you need to break the habit. An easy way to stop this is to award each team a goal or a penalty kick when they have earned three corners. (You can extend this rule to include throw-ins.)

Consequence rules add an extra degree of urgency to a game. When the amount of time that you play is directly related to how well you play, you tend to play a little harder. And in "Winners Stay," it's common to see the team that's sitting out analyzing their last match and making plans to avoid the same fate again. Or, if one team is dominating the games the other teams can get themselves up to knock them out — real grudge matches can develop.

Play with the Ball

As important as the ball is to soccer, it has to be the most neglected element in the game. A club may go to extraordinary lengths to get and maintain its fields and may spend too much money on uniforms. But just try to find a pump at practice! Training with under-inflated balls simply sets your team up for a problem later on. When the kids arrive at a game and find they have to play with one that more closely resembles a cannon ball, it can be intimidating. It can destroy their first touch, and start them thinking about the ball instead of the game. Always carry a pump and a few valve needles to practice and make sure that the balls are properly inflated.

Having an ample supply of balls is essential if you're going to play New Ball In. Some strategically placed shaggers can help by retrieving the loose ones and getting them back to the starting point for the game. By keeping these extra balls on hand and in the correct location, you can keep the pace of the game very high.

Keeping all that in mind, there will be times you'll want to change the composition of the ball to meet specific needs. Because most soccer balls meet FIFA's standards, they are very similar; you'll need to use another type of ball.

- **Futsal ball:** With vanishing green space, wet weather and closed fields, coaches are constantly trying to figure out where they can train. A quick look at public schools and parks will reveal a wealth of hard court opportunities. Tennis courts, basketball courts and school blacktops provide an almost weather proof playing surface. The problem with these areas is the surface is too fast — a regular ball will roll into the next county. That's where a futsal ball comes into play. It's a dead ball, so it has very little bounce and is difficult to get off of the ground. Futsal, recognized by FIFA is a five-a-side form of soccer played on a hard court, and its ball is made for exactly these conditions. Every coach should have at least two Futsal balls so that the practice can still go on in case the fields are closed.

- **Volleyball:** Some coaches will deflate a regular soccer ball when introducing children to heading, but this doesn't give the child the actual feel of a real ball. A volleyball is a good alternative at this stage. Because it's lighter than a soccer ball it can be properly inflated giving a more realistic feel in the early stages of learning. For the u-youngs a volleyball can also be an alternative to the standard size three. The larger, lighter ball is easier to track and manipulate and can be a useful aid in the early stages of skill development.

- **Futebol:** Futebols are the playground ball of South America and they're what the youngest children of Brazil learn to play soccer with. Made out of a dense rubber, they are very lively over short distances, but they don't travel too far — just like those red playground balls we used in elementary school. They duplicate the characteristics of a bad field where the ball is always bouncing slightly and can be a little difficult to control. After spending some time with these, first touch ball control becomes second nature.

> **So how can you tell when you have the game right? When you watch, it will be "just hot enough." The tempo of the game will be high enough to offer the kids a challenge, yet slow enough that they can play. This will help to keep them engaged and concentrating but not overwhelmed.**

Chapter 3

Soccer by Numbers

Before we get into the numbers game, we'll take a short look at how they're organized. It will help you understand small-sided games' place in the larger picture of 11-a-side soccer. After all, they're supposed to be the primary tool for getting kids onto the big field.

Think Thirds

Although the field is divided in half, you need to think in terms of thirds, Diagram 3-1. The area around your goal is your defensive third (called the back third) and the area around the opponent's goal is your attacking third (called the top third). The space in between is the middle third. Your opponent's thirds will be opposite yours: Your back/defensive third will be his front/attacking; your top/attacking third will be his back/defending.

Despite the labels, you don't 'just defend' around your own goal or 'just attack' around your opponents. When you have possession of the ball in your defensive third, it is not a defensive area for you at all. It's the staging area for your build up — it just happens to be a long way from the opponent's goal. And at the other end you need to defend effectively as well. You wouldn't pass up the opportunity to tackle an opponent in their penalty area.

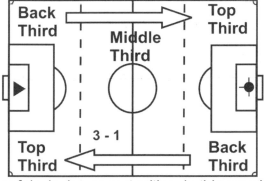

Thinking this way is useful when you're considering the risk to return, styles and the phases of play. In your back third any mistake can carry a high penalty, it's the area of a high risk to return. Therefore, you base your decisions and actions on the low-risk principle of safety first. At the other end of the field, the top third, there is less to risk and so you look for a higher return. Your decisions and actions will reflect this. In fact, playing too safely, losing opportunities, in this area is as detrimental as taking unnecessary risks in the back third.

It's the middle third that can drive coaches crazy. Youth soccer tends to ignore or misuse this area; teams go directly from the "safety-first zone" into the "all-or-nothing zone" when they cross midfield. Using the middle third as an area to hold the ball and build up the attack requires patience and good judgment. (Building up the attack, attacking and defending are the phases of play. While you can "build up your attack" anywhere on the field the middle third offers the most space, time and the most acceptable risk.) This is the area where no situation is all black or all white, and decisions are not going to be so clear-cut.

The Importance of Lines

Soccer teams are organized to meet certain requirements through a division of tasks among the players. This represents an attempt to balance the conflicting demands made by the principles of play. While a number of variables will affect the way you organize the team, there is one constant: The team's organization begins with the lines.

Consider the lines as a skeleton giving the team its shape. In 11-a-side soccer there are usually four, Diagram 3-2: Goalkeeper, back players, midfielders and top players. Because they have fewer players, small-sided games may only need two or three lines. The smaller games, 3v3 and 4v4, are based more on shapes, triangles and diamonds then actual lines. These shapes play a major role later on in 11-a-side soccer.

The team's lines help give the coach and player's their spatial orientation on the field. They are a way to bind the players together, providing reference points for the correct distance and angles. The lines provide each player with a context to interpret messages like "too far," "too close," "straight to," "diagonal from," "right," "left," "center," "in front of," "behind" and so on. Without a structure, the lines, these words are vague and ambiguous and that's a big step towards chaos and "amoeba ball."

Developing the Lines, Building the Structure

It's the space between and inside the lines that is of interest here, because when the spacing isn't right the organization breaks down. The team can no longer perform its basic functions effectively, and the game becomes a series of disjointed individual actions. Effective communication within and between the lines is essential to playing better soccer. (This is the problem when youth coaches complain that their kids can't retain their team shape. The distance and angles between the players is wrong and team cohesion breaks down.)

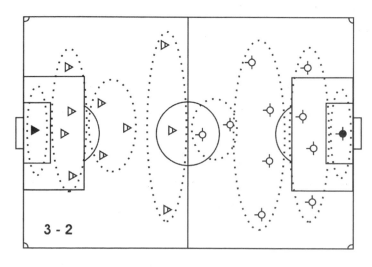

3 - 2

Diagram 3-2 shows two different ways to organize a team for the eleven a side game. The triangles are playing a 1-4-3-3 organization: a goalkeeper, four back players, three midfielders and three top players. Circles are playing a 1-4-4-2: a goalkeeper, four back players, four midfielders and two top players. These alignments can tell you, in a general way, about the basic tasks that the players have and how each team might approach the game.

For example, when the triangles play with three top players, while the circles only commit two real strikers, the triangles will probably take a more aggressive approach to the match while the circles will be expecting to gain an advantage in midfield. This example also illustrates one of the limitations about the lines. You can only have so many field players, so an extra player in one line has to come from another. When the triangles opt to play with three players up top, they must sacrifice a player from one of the other lines. In this case from the midfield which leaves them playing 3v4 there against the circles. On the other hand, two of the back players for the triangles will be unemployed unless they push up into the midfield to find their own opponent. These types of trade offs are common and must be accounted for in the distribution of tasks and in the teams plan.

Lines in Small-Sided Games

The lines in small-sided games, 5v5 and above, generally have two or three players. A two-player line will concentrate in the center of the field, which allows the players to support each other. It also means the line won't give the team much width for the build-up or the attack.

A two-player back line is vulnerable when the attack builds up on the flanks. If one defender moves out to put pressure on the attacker, the second defender has to choose between being close enough to supply cover and staying in the center. Choose the former and the center is left open. Choose the latter and deal with the gap between the two defenders. This problem is compounded when there is a second attacker in the center of the field. Another problem with a two-player back line appears when one of the players moves forward, for example after they win a tackle. If the team subsequently loses the ball, there's only one player left back and the team is open to the counterattack. Finally, two players mean that there is a right and a left but no center. This leaves a seam that can result in one of those "I thought you had him moments." If you're going to use two players in the back line, make sure they are very good, mobile players and that they communicate well. They will have a lot of responsibility.

Three players in the back offer's much greater safety. The line can shift and cover the space from the sideline to the center of the field. If one player moves forward, there are still two back reducing the threat from a counterattack. This allows each player greater freedom to move forward. Finally a three-player line makes one player responsible for the center of the field, which reduces confusion.

Think of it this way: Your attack starts at the point and moment you win the ball. When a defender has to chase back towards their goal and wins the ball facing that way, they have little chance for a quick counterattack. Or, if they win the ball in their penalty area, they'll be starting their attacks a long way from the opponent's goal. With this in mind, three defenders are more likely to hold the opponents in their own half and win the ball facing the other team's goal. They'll start the attacks in a stronger position and closer to their target. Three defenders can provide a more offensive line than two.

Two players up top spells 'counterattack.' They'll play primarily in the center and closely support each other. One should push up on the last defender and threaten the space behind the opponents. The other will play a little further back looking to link up with the back players. This means that most of the passes from the back will be into the center of the field to one of the two top players.

After a while, the center of the field will get pretty crowded. Eventually, someone will need to try to pass the ball out on the wing. At that point, the question becomes who should chase it — one of the strikers or someone from the back line. Either way the balance in the team will be affected.

Three players up top can really spread the opponents back line. In fact, that's the hallmark of the playmaking style. Just by virtue of being there, the three-player top line forces the opponents to cover more space, creating more attacking opportunities, e.g. bigger gaps between the defenders and more 1v1's. That said you run the danger of the top players forgetting they also must play defense, neglecting to close into the center or drop back to help when the opponents have possession. If the top players think that their job is one-dimensional — i.e., get the ball and cross it or score— whenever you lose the ball you'll be players down against the opponents.

Principles of Play: In Possession

When in possession of the ball, teams can use their organization to create space inside an opponent's line, between their lines or both. (Match the teams in Diagram 3-2 against each other and compare how each team would respond to the others attacking options. Invariably, players from one line will be expected to push up, or drop back to another line.)

- **Penetration & Depth:** One way to create space is to stretch the opponents from end to end. This means that at least one attacking player will need to play higher, up top, while the other one plays deeper, farther back. The top player's job is to threaten the space behind the opponents while the deeper player holds other defenders in place. In soccer-speak: The top player satisfies the principle of penetration and the deeper one provides depth. These players can be in the same or different lines.

- **Principle of Width:** You can also stretch the defending team from side to side. By playing at least one player wide on each flank, your team meets the principle of width in attack. When attackers threaten to go around a line, the defenders can be stretched moving across the field to meet the threat. If they don't work as a unit, the gaps that develop between the defenders can give the attackers an advantage. Unlike penetration and depth, where the attacking players can be in different lines, the most effective way to use width is when the attacking players are in, or move into, the same line, i.e. the triangles top line or the circles midfield line in diagram 3-2.

- **Principle of Mobility:** Whenever attackers switch positions, defenders are forced to make on the spot decisions. Do they go with the player or stay in the vacated space? If they go, how far should they go? The principle of mobility, attackers changing places, can cause a moment's hesitation by a defender — a mistake that may be all the attackers need to strike. Attackers don't own a position. They merely occupy and play from one.

The Principles of Play: Opponents in Possession

Defensively teams want to limit the available space that the opponents have to work in. They can't do that if they can't control their own space.

- **Applying pressure:** It's the single most important defensive principle. Simply put, someone needs to mark the player with the ball. However, where and how aggressively you apply pressure is open to debate. If you are ahead by a couple of goals late in the game you can play a low-pressure game, only pressurizing players if they pose a direct threat. If you're behind by a goal with 10 minutes to play you'll need to force the opponents into an error and will play a high-pressure game.

- **The Principle of Cover or Support**: Defenders are human and the pressurizing player will get beaten from time to time. They'll need a free, second defender close by and goal side to immediately reapply pressure to the attacker with the ball. The principle of cover or support works well in theory, but is very hard to carry out in small-sided games. The problem is that in small-sided games like 2v2, 3v3, 4v4 and even up to 8v8 everyone has an immediate opponent. This means that a player must leave his or her opponent to supply the cover and that leaves their player open to become a free attacker. The solution creates a new problem that we'll address below.

- **Balance in Defense**: The distance between the players in each line is referred to as balance in defense. Simply put, you don't want everyone on the same side of the field as the ball. Your opponents will be able to go around your entire defense in a single pass across the field.

- **Depth in Defense**: When the defense cannot be beaten in a single action, you have depth in defense. It is lacking when, for example, two defenders are so close together that an attacker beats both of them with the same dribble, or the fullback stands at midfield and the opponents play the ball into the space between him and the goalkeeper. Like balance in defense poor depth can be the result of too much, or too little space.

- **The Principle of Concentration**: If there are enough players in the defensive scheme to handle the current situation, the principle of concentration is in play. As a general rule, defenders should out number attackers; in small-sided games, i.e. up to 8v8, having free defenders is only possible when you leave the least dangerous opponent unmarked. That means leaving the attackers behind or farthest away from the ball free. By figuring out which attacker is least likely to do any real damage defenders can achieve a numerical superiority goal side of the ball. However, when defenders are skilled in the craft of individual defending fewer players are needed to fulfill this principle. (This in turn frees up more players for attacking roles.)

In effect, attackers will try to disrupt and disorganize their opponent's structure, while defenders try to keep their organization intact and not allow individual players to become isolated. In turn they will actively try to disrupt the attackers plans. This dance begins with the team's organization and continues as players use their individual and collective skills. Looking at it this way, you can see soccer as a game between opposing forces, opposites really. Each team tries to give their opponents unsolvable problems while, at the same time, solving the problems the opponents dish out. Without the correct organization, individuals will not be able to play to the best of their capability. In other words, their ability to play their best soccer will be hampered and that weakens the team.

Small-Sided Games 1v1 through 8v8

As we look at 1v1 through 8v8, each level will build on and incorporate the lessons of the preceding one, while laying the groundwork for the next. This way you'll come away with a better understanding of what the "small-sided" means in small-sided games.

It's All or Nothing: 1v1

Being comfortable on both sides of 1v1 is essential for players who are trying to reach a higher level of play. At the very least, players shouldn't lose the ball when they're in possession and should be difficult to beat when they're not. The question is not the importance of 1v1, but finding the most effective way to teach it.

In the P.E. model 1v1 is taught in three separate stages. On the attacking end, players learn some moves, dribble through cones or play keep-away games in a grid. Then they play some 1v1 with goals so they can use their new moves on an actual defender, and finally they end up with a small game. On the defensive side, they might get some theory, i.e. a lecture along with a demonstration, the 1v1 stage and finally the small-sided game.

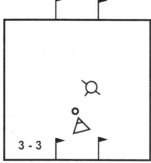

But a downside to 1v1 is that many games are a one-shot, winner-take-all event, Diagram 3-3. Once a player loses the ball in a tackle, or gets beaten, the game is over and outside of scoring, learning has stopped. Also, neither player can expect any help, and this can result in a stalemate. Both players can bide their time simply waiting for their opponent to commit an error.

And so, the game can come to a standstill. A common remedy to this is to encourage the defender to be overly aggressive and "force the situation" and for the attacker to "take them on" to "Go! Go! Go!" But forcing the situation this way is unrealistic; it reinforces frantic football. The actual game, the situation that the players are facing, doesn't call for that type of response. Patience, to find the correct moment to act, is what is required of both players. They are being robbed of an opportunity to work through the decision process themselves; they're looking for the correct moment with an artificial game clock. It's an example of adult micromanaging, and creates more puppets then players.

Finally, if there's too great a difference in the players' abilities, the weaker player gets run over and fails to offer any real resistance. Then the weaker player becomes demoralized, the better one becomes bored, and neither benefits from the game. 1v1s are most effective when the players are close to the same level and motivation. When you see a real battle between the players taking place you have success.

Teamwork at its Smallest: 2v2

Consider some of the differences between 1v1 and 2v2:

- 2v2 includes the element of cooperation, offering children the opportunity to work with a teammate. 1v1 does not.

- 2v2 includes all of the smallest basic forms. 1v1, 2v1 and 1v2 situations are all part of 2v2. Learning to read for the 1v1 opportunity can be learned best when it's contained inside of a bigger game. That means players learn to look for the situation instead of having it presented to them.

- The team in possession during a 2v2 receives the same opportunities to practice all of the dribbling techniques and moves as 1v1 plus quick, short passing actions. Individual defending can be supplemented with learning to intercept a pass and closing down defenders receiving them.

- 2v2 allows players to learn how to 'sell the pass, make the dribble' or 'sell the dribble, make the pass' to beat their opponent. They can learn how to disguise their intentions, an important dribbling skill. Because 1v1 only offers dribbling as an attacking option, it has no way for children to learn this.

- 2v2 games can last longer than 1v1. After a turnover the additional player can slow the opponent's counterattack and keep the game going. This creates more moments of transition within the game (another key learning point) and helps keep the level of concentration higher and longer.

Developing the skills for effective teamwork is a lifelong task. With 2v2 games, that starts from the beginning: They'll need to establish who's in charge, than agree to a plan. 2v2 games, especially mini-tournaments where there is more pressure, provide a good laboratory to see how well players work together. They provide room and opportunities for self-expression and cooperative problem solving, and children can develop and try out their own ideas to meet the problems they are facing.

After they decide on their plan, hold them accountable to it. In 2v2, it only concerns "you and me" — about as simple as it gets. Many children will favor a democratic approach, i.e. sharing tasks, which is fine. However this can slow play and result in missed opportunities, because the children are too busy solving the problem of being fair and taking turns rather than winning the next point. Make this situation one of your teaching points. Ask the children, "Does this help you to play better?" A question like this can prompt them to take the game, the situation and the resources into account when they plan their strategy. However, if they measure success by being fair instead of expedient then that's their decision and you can accept it. In their own way they have achieved success.

2v2, like 1v1, offers a choice between the playmaking and the counter-attacking styles of play. The decision affects the team's approach to the game, and the players' positions on the field. Both players have to agree to the style and the place to start is with the team's defensive plan and structure.

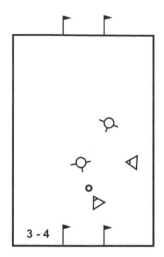

In Diagram 3-4, the two defenders have agreed to use the play making style. Both have moved far up field in an effort to hold the attackers in their own half. They are in agreement as to how they'll approach the situation when the opponents have possession. They want to play as close to the opponent's goal as possible, even when they don't have the ball. This way, when they win the ball they don't have far to go.

This is a very aggressive approach to the game and takes a positive, can do mentality. Setbacks are only seen as temporary and the risk is worth the return.

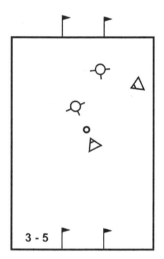

In Diagram 3-5, the defenders have adopted the counterattacking style, closer to their own goal and conceding the attackers half. Again, the two defenders are in agreement about how to approach the situation. This is a more conservative, safety-first approach. It requires patience and when they win the ball they will have farther to go to the opponents goal. This approach doesn't work when you're behind or the opponent isn't willing or able to carry the attack to you.

Many young players don't recognize the importance of playing together and become separated from one another. One player will charge about the field while the other guards the goal. This is an inefficient use of their resources, each other, and makes for a lot of unnecessary work.

2v2 is good for learning how to play as the second attacker, when to move ahead of the ball and when to stay behind it. After all, if you're teammate has the ball you're the only player who can offer any help. The situation forces the player without the ball to answer, "When should I go ahead of my teammate?" Going ahead at the wrong moment is even worse then not going ahead at all.

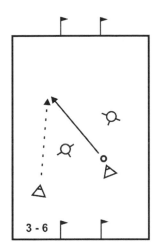

In Diagram 3-6, the attacker without the ball sees there's space behind the two defenders and that his teammate will be able to deliver a pass there. This is a good time to make a run forward, especially if the attacker with the ball can catch the defenders ball watching.

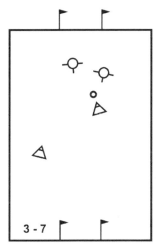

Diagram 3-7 shows a situation where it is not a good time to run forward. There is very little space behind the defenders, and the player with the ball is getting some pressure. The second attacker is already in a good supporting position and should simply hold there and wait to see what develops. Even if the attacker with the ball loses possession, the second attacker is behind the ball and in a position to delay the counterattack.

The Smallest Size for Shape: 3v3

3v3 builds naturally on the lessons of 2v2, and introduces the concept of shape. Players move from a straight line between two points to fluid triangles. This is a major step up in development as the problems and solutions have gone from a simple "you and me" to "you, me and what's-his-name." This 50 percent increase in the number of players can slow down the speed of the game dramatically as the children process additional information and options.

When their team has possession, the two players without the ball have to solve the problem of knowing where the other one is as they watch the player with the ball. In the beginning, they may move into the same space, thinking the same thoughts, unaware of each other and generally get in each other's way. The player with the ball may fixate on one teammate, ignoring the other. That player will find it difficult to shift attention between the two. For each player, information overload will be an issue at the outset.

When the opposing team has possession, defenders must settle on who will pressurize the player with the ball and what the other two players should do. There will be several options available, so expect the initial decision-making process to proceed slowly and erratically.

3v3 can introduce the concept of specialization, the division of tasks. For example, if a team chooses to leave one player back to fill the basic defensive tasks, it leaves the other two free to play farther up field and take primary responsibility for attacking functions. This, in turn, frees the 'defender' even more to concentrate on staying behind the ball. The team functions are simplified and use everyone's energy and talent more efficiently. The players run less and get a higher return on their efforts.

Specialization is an important element in team building. The team elects to divide basic tasks in such a way that they will be playing with a clear shape and rationale. The organization has meaning to achieve the objective. The 'specialist' in 3v3 will hold a central position, and the other two will orient on that player's right and left regardless if the central player is up top or at the back.

Sometimes you'll observe problems that don't stem from the plan but from how it's executed. It takes a higher level of concentration and discipline to accept responsibility and children can mistake their new found 'role' for a license to only play as an attacker or defender. They misread the fine print in the agreement and fail to fulfill part of the contract. The defender who only defends makes little or no contribution to the team when they are in possession. This can leave the team playing 2v3 when they have the ball, not good odds in the long run. This is a common problem that's learned young, and shows up even in 11v11.

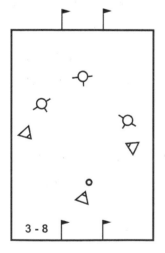

3 - 8

Diagram 3-8 shows a common 3v3 problem. The attacker is coming out unopposed, their immediate opponent dropping back behind his or her teammates to act as a 'sweeper.' This allows the attacker to dribble straight between the other defenders and attack the 'sweeper' or to join forces with a teammate and create a 2v1 on a flank. The sweeper is only able to see the problem from a limited perspective, "Protect the goal and cover the space behind your teammates" and fails to see that she can better protect the goal by pushing farther out to apply pressure to the attacker. She should let her teammates do their jobs, neutralizing their immediate opponents themselves.

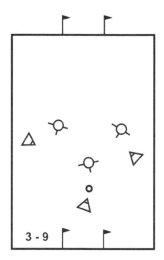

Diagram 3-9 shows the correct solution, man to man marking. Now, the player with the ball is under immediate pressure. While this sacrifices the cover behind the other two defenders the principle of pressurizing is more important at the moment. This illustrates the limitation in the defensive principles and small-sided games. Defenders must choose which principle, in this case pressure or cover, is most important and which to ignore.

Real Soccer: 4v4

If you coach children over the age of eight and only want to play one game go with the basic game and 4v4. 4v4 is the smallest form for "real" soccer, because all of the principles of play are used, and every player has a defined role. In terms of learning soccer by playing soccer, this form is universally regarded as the best.

The standard shape for 4v4 is a diamond, which leaves less open space on the field than 3v3 and presents a new problem for the players. 3v3 gives players the luxury of being able to escape trouble by dribbling, running or passing the ball into the vacant space. There's always some open area they can take advantage of through an individual action. But in 4v4 the escape is harder, because a teammate and an opponent are occupying the formerly vacant space. More then 3v3, 4v4 requires players to create space for their teammates as well as themselves.

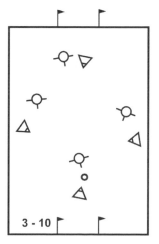

Compare the availability of open space between 3v3 and 4v4 in diagrams 3-9 and 3-10. 3v3 games can flow in and out of the open area, but 4v4 requires a more disciplined approach. While the game can flow, each position is usually occupied and this restricts the players' freedom to move. 4v4 requires a much higher level of cooperation between all of the players. In order to use space teams will need to create it.

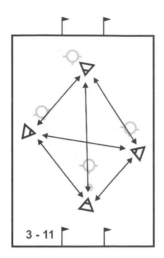

3 - 11

Diagram 3-11 illustrates how the diamond shape develops when each player accepts a role. One up, one back, one left and one right: It's the best way to cover the field. In 3v3 one of these roles will always be unfilled. Anyone can slide into the empty position, which simply moves the empty position to a new area. In this sense, 3v3 is much more dynamic than 4v4, requiring less discipline and more opportunism. 3v3 problems are solved more often with technical answers than in 4v4, where tactics play a greater role. In the former, players are dealing with a single triangle, one "me, you and what's his name." Decisions can be made faster. In 4v4 every player is involved in three different 'triangles,' Diagram 3-11 at all times and there's a fourth that they're not even a part of. That's a lot more to work through. When you keep in mind that when you're dealing with six, seven and eight year olds, with limited familiarity to small-sided games, you get an idea how much harder 4v4 is then 3v3. Without a strong base of experience the number of options in 4v4 can be overwhelming. This raises the stress level that initiates the fight or flight response and children either shut down or go it alone. The only practical way to gain experience with small-sided games is to play small-sided games. There simply aren't any short cuts.

First Duplicate Task: 5v5

Adding a goalkeeper to 4v4 and calling it 5v5 doesn't effectively change the tasks or relationships of the players on the field. The four field players will still play in a diamond and have the same tasks and responsibilities as in 4v4. However, 5v5 with only field players presents a whole new set of problems, because one of the basic roles will have to be duplicated. This impacts all of the players.

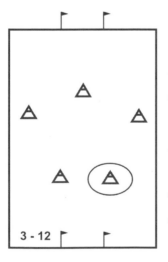

3 - 12

In Diagram 3-12, the fifth player (circled) has been given a defensive role as a second sweeper. In spite of what you might think this actually produces a stronger attacking formation. The midfielders don't have to be as concerned with their defensive tasks and can afford to play farther forward. It also means that the team has two defenders — a right and a left — rather than a single central defender and that change's the job description of the original sweeper. He or she will only be responsible for half the field. Finally, with the two midfielders playing so far forward the top player's space will be more limited. This alignment works well when you are the stronger team and you know that you can play in the opponent's half. That is, use the playmaking style.

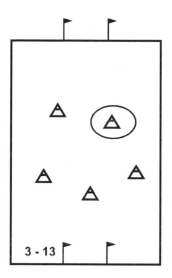

In Diagram 3-13, the fifth player has been added alongside the top player, which limits the space and opportunities the midfielders have to move forward. They'll end up playing more in line with the sweeper and creating a stronger defensive alignment. The two strikers would work together to solve most of their problems by themselves while the opportunities and space for the midfielders and sweeper to move forward will be limited. This would be a good system if you were playing a strong opponent and wanted to concentrate on using the counterattack, or at least the back three to hold the opponents in their half. Pulling one of the forwards back alongside the central defender, essentially a 4-1 could strengthen the defense even more but at the expense of the attack.

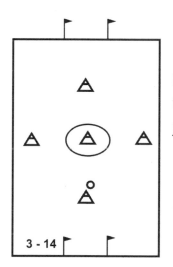

If the fifth player were added to the midfield it would be in the center, Diagram 3-14. This arrangement offers the team the chance to move quickly between the previous two formations. The fifth player, call him a central midfielder, would have to be very intelligent and active. He would use this position as a starting point to join in the attack or to cover his teammate's forward runs.

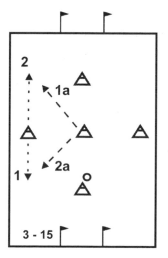

Diagram 3-15 shows the sweeper in possession and the left midfielder dropping back, run 1. The center midfielder moves over to occupy the vacated space, run 1a. This helps to restore the balance in the team and clears the space between the sweeper and the top player for a through pass.

A second option shows the left midfielder moving forward, run 2. This time the center midfielder covers the space that he just left, run 2a.

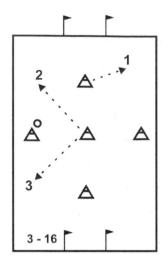

In Diagram 3-16, with the ball on the flank, the top player has cleared out the attacking space with a run to the right, 1. The center midfielder can move forward into the open space, run 2, or drop behind the left midfielder, run 3, and let him go forward on his own.

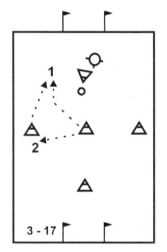

In Diagram 3-17 the top player has possession and is under pressure. The center midfielder could move forward to support him, run 1, or drop behind the left midfielder, run 2, if he makes the run forward.

These are just a few of the possibilities that the center midfielder has. The 1-3-1 is a very dynamic and complex system, more so then the 2-3 or 3-2. The player in the center midfield role would have to be aware of everyone around them and have a keen sense of timing. The level of understanding and communication in the team has to be very high because the demands placed by the principle of mobility leaves a lot of room for mistakes. It's important to make the run but, it's no good going too early, too late or when someone else is already there.

Introducing the Goalkeeper: 6v6

The next level, 6v6, is usually when the goalkeeper is introduced. (See Chapter 2.) In conjunction with the unique rules for goalkeepers, field players will continue playing by the principles of 5v5 outlined above. It is important that the goalkeeper plays as a part of the team. They should assume the role of a sweeper at every chance and help the team to establish a numerical advantage. If you are using 6v6 without goalkeepers for a training game just apply the following guidelines for the field players in 7v7.

Introducing Wingers: 7v7

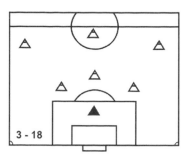

In Diagram 3-18, we see a 1-3-3 system, a common lineup for 7v7. Its strength results from where the two winger's play — very high and wide, providing width against the opposing team's back line. This creates space for the center forward and 1v1 opportunities for all three top players. The back players can mark man-to-man or divide the field into three zones. The goalkeeper will play as a sweeper behind the backs. This system works well when you know that you will have a lot of ball possession and can dictate how the game will go, i.e. you'll use the playmaking style of play.

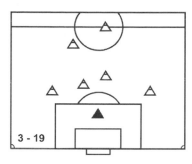

Here, Diagram 3-19, you see a 1-4-2. It's useful when you're not sure about the opponent and want to build in a little extra safety. Bringing back one of the top players requires the remaining two to move closer to each other and play in the center of the field. Here the deepest player threatens the back of the opponent's defense, while the second player looks for gaps to exploit forward and also has to check back to receive passes from the back players.

The attack will build up through the center of the field, and wing play will be based more on opportunity than on design. Any one of the four back players can move forward and you will still have three defenders. However, it's a long run to get past the top players, and an even longer run to get back. The two central defenders can give each other some depth and, since you're committing an extra player to the defensive line, supply cover to the outside backs. Once again, the goalkeeper acts as a sweeper behind the back line.

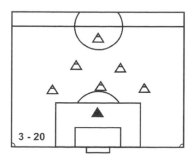

Diagram 3-20: This Christmas tree system, 1-3-2-1, is the ultimate for 7v7 counterattacking. It also uses four actual lines, a rarity in 7v7. It works best when the opponent wants, or has, to carry the attack to you. The structure invites the opposing back players to come forward into open space. But the farther they go, the more crowded the space becomes. Eventually they will lose the ball and the lone striker has a 1v1 at midfield. The two midfielders must push forward quickly and, for a brief moment, try to gain a numerical advantage. Once possession is lost they'll retreat back to their defensive positions and wait for the next opportunity. Patience, organization, staying within your tasks and a fast, technically competent striker are the keys to this system's success.

Beginning of Four-Line Play:8v8

The extra player in 8v8 offers more opportunities to use four-line systems.

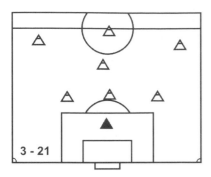

In Diagram 3-21, we have a 1-3-1-3 organization. Just like the 1-3-3 in Diagram 3-18 it allows for two wingers and a central striker who are responsible for the team's width and penetration. But now they have a center half between them and the back line. This player will need to be a dominant personality, capable of covering a lot of ground, who can win the ball and play through 180 degrees. The center half will combine with the striker and act as the link between the top and back players. He or she should be able to reach either wing with a pass. It's also very important that the back players close up into midfield but not so much that they crowd the center midfielder. Allowing too much space between the backs and top players can isolate the four outside players, and create a situation in which the central midfielder is easily bypassed.

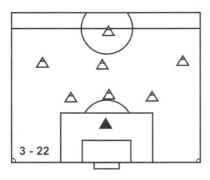

Diagram 3-22 shows what happens when the wingers drop back and the system becomes 1-3-3-1. The defensive scheme has been reinforced, but the striker will do a lot of playing solo. And when the outside midfielders make their runs forward they'll be starting 10-15 yards farther back. When you remember that they'll have to cover the same distance on their recovery run, you can appreciate why they will be a little slower after the sixth time they've gone forward. (It's even harder if they make the run and don't get the ball.)

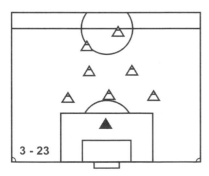

Diagram 3-23 shows how 1-3-2-2 solves the problem of supporting the striker, but still leaves you in the counterattacking scheme. When the center midfielder pushes up and takes on a more attacking role, it empties the center of the field, forcing the left and right midfielders to move closer together and concedes the space on the outside. Without any real width in the attack, the opponent's defensive line can concentrate on stopping the two strikers. Attacks will have to be lightning quick and be built around the top players' individual technical abilities.

Playing With Two Systems

It would be a mistake to leave the numbers game thinking that you only play in one system. In fact most teams play two. One, when they have possession and the other when the opponents have possession. For example, a team playing 8-a-side could adopt the 1-3-1-3 system, Diagram 3-21 when they have possession. As soon as they lose possession they fall back to the 1-3-3-1 in Diagram 3-22. The change is built into the basic tasks of the wingers/flank midfielders.

This type of play isn't seen too often in youth soccer outside of the "amoeba system." The rigid application of a single system of play can act as a restraint on the players. They become glued to their spot, waiting for the game to come to them. The system should serve the team, it's needs and qualities and not the other way around.

Level by Level: 1v1 Thru 8v8

As we follow the progression from 1v1 to 8v8, you can see how each level builds on elements of the preceding one and prepares players for the next. Small-sided games are dependent on each individual's choices and actions. Everyone on your team needs to at least be comfortable and competent in 1v1. When you consider the number of situations on the field where two players will have to work closely together you can appreciate how important 2v2 is. And finally when you look at the diagrams and see the prevalence of triangles and diamonds it becomes clear how important it is for children to learn how to use 3v3 and 4v4 to achieve their objectives. Distance, angles, shapes and timing are tools, and learning to use them properly is as important as learning any technique, so time spent in small-sided games is never wasted.

And that's one of the strongest arguments in support of small-sided games: They help children learn how to play soccer, the whole game, by playing it in different, simplified forms. As you expose them to a variety of games, they can learn the ideas and master techniques necessary to progress to the next level. No matter what the size of your competitive match, small-sided games provide plenty of learning opportunities for the full 11-a-side game.

Uneven Numbers Bridge the Levels

It would be nice if all you had to do were to move, carefree, straight through the numbers. But then there's the principle of resistance, and that's where using uneven numbers in training can really help. Your players might have a pretty good idea how to play at a certain level, like 3v3, but the new demands of the higher level, such as 4v4 initially prove to be too much. Lower the opponent's resistance by removing one player and playing 4v3. The four players can get used to the new demands while playing with less opposition. (In this case you'll want to coach the four-player- team.) When you see the four-player team is meeting the demands of the new level you can bring the fourth opponent back in. Now the teams are back level at 4v4 and the players have a whole new set of problems to solve.

Neutral Players Benefit the Team in Possession

Neutral players give the team in possession an advantage in numbers. Neutral players, or chameleons, change colors by playing only with the team in possession. When they receive a pass from a Blue player they play for blue. When they receive a pass from Red they play for red. They have no defensive responsibilities. They never intercept a pass or make a tackle.

Neutral players can be used in several different ways. They can be an individual or another team. They can play on the field, off of the field or both. As we saw in Chapter 2 they can even play as goals.

Even you can get into the act as a neutral player. By taking on this role yourself you are able to have a tremendous influence in the game. You can help children who are struggling by getting them out of jams while at the same time help the better players by combining with them to play a faster game than their teammates may be capable of.

Two things you want to consider when playing as a neutral player: First, use the role to get an idea across, and then get out of the game. Second, don't play as a neutral player if you will become a problem yourself. It can adversely affect your credibility if you break what you're trying to fix.

Diagram 3-24 shows a 2v2 + NP, or 3v2 both ways. Both the Triangles and the Circles enjoy the advantage that the neutral player gives them when they have the ball and suffer when the opponents have it.

Since neutral players don't have any defensive responsibilities they should spend most of their time on the flanks. It's pretty ugly when a neutral player plays as a sweeper, loses the ball in a tackle and then gets to score in the open goal because they just became the opponent's center forward!

Too often coaches get hung up on what is the best system to use. The simple fact of the matter is that it should always give your players the best chance to play to their strengths while minimizing their weaknesses. To do this you'll need to have a good understanding of their qualities as they match up against their opponents as well as their motivation for the match. While there are certain favorite systems you'll tailor your own through the distribution of tasks. This will give your players their best chance of success.

Chapter 4

First Step to the Task: Choose the Style of Play

Before you decide on what tasks players should have you need to choose a style of play that suits the situation they are about to face. Consider this analogy:

Muhammad Ali knew that George Foreman would bring the fight to him when they met in Zaire in 1974, and he reasoned that standing in the center of the ring and going toe to toe with the larger and more powerful Foreman might not be a good idea. So he introduced rope-a-dope. Ali laid back and absorbed an ineffective attack. Then, after a few rounds of this, when his opponent was tired and frustrated, Ali unleashed his own attack. Foreman couldn't cope with Ali's bunker defense and walked right into his plan. On the other hand when Mike Tyson was in his prime he had a more straightforward approach: Immediately crush the opponent. Tyson was always in control, and both he and his opponents knew it. The examples of these two fighters show how you can use different tactics and still be successful. Soccer teams need to think along the same lines, varying their strategies according to the situation they are about to face.

Choosing a style begins with your prediction of the final result. If you think you'll win 4, 5 or 6-0 you have no troubles. You're Mike Tyson, in control and basically ignore what the opponent has to offer. The playmaking style is the way to go. You plan on playing in the opponent's half and having a lot of ball possession. You'll be able to dictate the tempo of the match.

But if you think you're going to be on the wrong end of 6–0, you better cover up and ride it out. Protect yourself and look for the opportunities to counter. You'll spend a lot of time backed up in your own half and starting your attacks close to your penalty area. When you do have possession you'll have to work quickly because you won't have the ball very long. The opponent will dictate how the game will go and you had better recognize that in your plan.

This is not saying that you'll be going out to lose. No team ever does that. Rather, simply take reality into account. Sure, on any given day any team can beat any other team. But this is today, and you need to consider probabilities, not possibilities. A good plan is essential to getting the most out of your team, and to be good, it has to be based on a realistic assessment of the two teams. Hope may spring eternal, but it's not a valid game-planning method.

The hard part is when you're looking at the 1–0 and 2–1 games. What do you do? Two equal teams, neither will dominate the other or maybe a little bit of both for short periods. The decision you and your players face is when to end one style and start the other. That's where your players come in. They are in the best place to decide when to take the game up a level or to regroup and simply hold on until the storm passes.

How the team approaches the game has a direct effect on every player's basic task. At a minimum, the choice determines where and how the team will organize the defense. And where you organize your defense is where you expect to begin your attacks. Choose the playmaking approach, and everybody is pushed up and expends a lot of energy to win the ball as close to the opponent's goal as possible. When counterattacking is the style, players will delay the opponents' build-up to buy time for the defense to organize closer to their own penalty area.

Your choice of style will allow you to highlight certain techniques and skills. It will also influence which system of play you'll use. Without agreement on what style of play the team will adopt players can't be held responsible for their positioning because they don't have the 'big picture' to guide them. A center forward in the counterattacking style approaches, and will behave differently in the game then one in the playmaking style.

4 - 1

Diagram 4-1 shows a team playing 8v8 in the playmaking style when the opponents have possession in their own half. Everyone pushes up. In this way, when the team wins the ball they don't have far to go to get at the opponents goal and they can keep the opponents under constant pressure in their own half. When done properly this is the most effective style because you're in control and can dictate the speed of the game. You are relying on your own qualities and not on what the opponent may or may not do.

Many youth teams try to use the playmaking style but fail to use the entire team. The goalkeeper stays to close to the penalty area, the fullbacks to close to the midfield line, the top players fail to track back to contribute defensively so the midfielders get to chase the ball around the rest of the field. The game comes down to who has the better athletes and which coach can shout, "hustle" or "pressure" the loudest. There is a noticeable disconnect between the players tasks and the teams plan. This style of play takes considerable courage and self-confidence. If even one player is lacking in this it's very difficult to pull off.

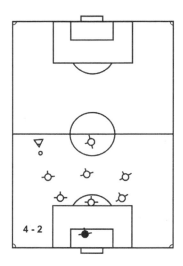

Diagram 4-2 shows how to set up the counter-attacking style defense and attack. Everyone comes back and the team concentrates in their half. The idea is to keep the opponents playing in front of you, limit the amount of open space behind you and to keep numbers up close to your penalty area. You'll guide or encourage the opponents into a mistake rather then trying to force the error. While this is stronger defensively, when you win the ball you'll have a longer way to go to reach your opponent's penalty area and likely won't maintain possession very long. This style works when you don't expect, or have to carry the game for any significant period. It doesn't work if the opponent won't come forward. (What would Ali have done if Foreman hadn't come after him?)

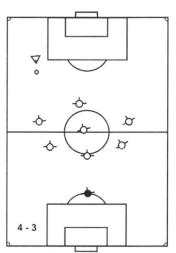

Diagram 4-3 shows a compromise between the two styles of play. The team concedes their top third, allowing the opponents to use it for their build up. The team concentrates their numbers in the middle third so they are close enough to their own penalty area that they can drop back if pressed, yet near enough to the opponents that, when the chance presents itself, they can press forward as a team. The key is that the distance between the lines is not too great. Too much or too little space between the lines makes effective defending difficult which, in turn, makes it harder to attack as well.

Tasks and Responsibilities

When we looked at how teams use their lines to create a structure (Chapter 3), we saw how the basic organization reflects the team's strategy for fulfilling its critical tasks. In doing so, the team is balancing the demands of the principles of play. Think of it this way, it's a matter of having the correct balance between attackers and defenders and you know its right when the team moves smoothly through the four main moments.

In a perfect world building your team would just be a matter of picking a system of play and then putting each player in a position. Your problems would be over and you could concentrate on the important things like the half-time snacks. Unfortunately, it's not a perfect world.

Players need to know more then just the name of the position that they occupy, e.g. center half. They need a job description that includes some basic details, e.g. to provide a link between the back and top players, to defend in the center of the field, to look for the opponents half clearances and so on. Each individual's responsibility has to tie back into larger needs — those of the line and the team. Your players must understand their job description in terms of the team's objectives.

Understanding a task is good, but it falls flat if you can't perform it. Countless times, a coach has to put a right-footed player on the left wing. Chances are that player won't be able to cross the ball and someone else has to pick up the slack or suffer the consequences. In this case it's the center forward who doesn't receive any quality crosses.

A chain is only as strong as its weakest link and the team's success boils down to each player filling their role. When one player fails on that level, it has a domino effect. A second player has to clean up the mess, and if that player's job suffers the problem falls to a third player, and so on down the line. The team is passing the problem on, not solving it.

Match your players as best you can to their best positions and if someone doesn't have the qualities for a particular job try to account for it in your plan. If you don't then the team structure will contain a built-in flaw, and you'll start off not firing on all cylinders.

After you select the best system for your personnel you're off and running. Nothing will stand in the way of your soccer machine. Yea, right! You're a youth coach, and youth coaches substitute players. You'll dismantle your front line — the one that worked so well for the first 15 minutes — and send two new wingers on the field, disrupting the center forward's groove until all three on the line adjust to each other and the game. Then it will be time to sub the center forward, and the wingers will have to adjust to their new target player. (We'll look at substituting, supply some guidelines and a form in Chapter 9.)

And remember the wingers that we took out earlier? Now you have them playing in the back line, a very different job description then their earlier one. Imagine going into work and having your job and work site completely changed every two hours. You're never in a job long enough to get the hang of it before you're told to pack up and move. You live in a perpetual state of orientation, where an abundance of enthusiasm has to make up for a lack of cohesion. It's frustrating, to say the least.

Basic tasks in 4v4

Since 4v4 is considered to be the smallest form of real soccer we'll take a look at how the basic tasks would be distributed inside the team in the two main moments, when the team has possession and when the opponents do. We'll address the supplemental tasks a little later.

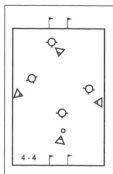

Own team in possession.

Tasks for the triangles as they bring the ball out.

Position	Basic Task(s)	Supplemental Task(s)
Sweeper	• Insure high quality distribution out of the back. • Do not give the ball away. • Support the other players from behind.	• Look for opportunities to join or move past the midfielders.
Midfielders	• Provide a link between the sweeper and striker and support both. • Create space by stretching the opponents across the field. • Create quality opportunities to score.	• Score Goals
Striker	• Score and set up goals. • To create space by holding the opposing sweeper deep. • Offer quality targets to teammates.	• Look for opportunities to switch positions with, or create space for teammates.

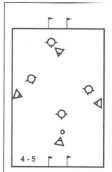

Opponents in possession.

Tasks for the circles as the triangles bring the ball out.

Position	Basic Task(s)
Striker	• To neutralize the opposing sweeper. • To disrupt distribution out of the back. • To track down any forward runs made by the sweeper.
Midfielders	• To neutralize their immediate opponent. • To provide cover to the striker. • To maintain positive numbers goal side of the ball.
Sweeper	• To neutralize the opposing striker. • To provide cover to the midfielders.

In some forms of 5v5, 6v6 and 7v7, when you only play with two lines, you lack an actual 'midfield' to link the top and back players. You can adjust for this in one or both of the lines. One or more players can assume the basic task of linking up with the other line. This can be a player from the back moving up or from the top dropping back, essentially playing an "unofficial" midfield role. Just keep an eye on them that they don't neglect their other basic tasks in the process.

Conflicts in the Basic Tasks

The above chart highlights an inherent conflict. Each player needs at least two basic tasks, one for when the team is in possession of the ball, and one for when the other team has it.

The basic task for the center forward whose team has possession is to threaten the back of the opponent's defense and score goals. But this doesn't apply when the opponents have the ball. Either the center forward needs a different task or the team will have to play without him until the next "We have the ball" moment. Extend this idea throughout every position in the team, and you'll easily see how teams are reduced to back players who only defend and attackers who only attack. Children often see their jobs in terms of their labels, attackers or defenders; it's black or white. This leaves them with a very limited view of their responsibilities where each has a job in a part of the game but few with a job in all of the game.

So we assign the center forward the basic task of marking the opposing sweeper whenever their team has the ball. This sounds like a reasonable request, because they are both in the same area of the field. Now the center forward has a job in two of the main moments, something to do when either team has the ball. The center forward has gone from being employed 40 percent of the time to working 80 percent of the time. Perfect, except for one thing: Attacking and defending principles are opposing forces and may require the center forward to be in two different places.

Depending on the moment, the center forward must be in a specific place to do his or her job properly. When the team has possession that means playing deep and trying to score goals and this might take them away from the sweeper. When the other team has the ball it means staying goal side of the sweeper, keeping a close eye on them. No matter which side of the ball possession question a player is on, what's the correct spot in one moment may be incorrect as soon as the ball changes hands. It takes a while for children to appreciate that, to understand that while they have not done anything wrong themselves, circumstances have changed and made them wrong.

This is where the two transition moments, winning the ball and losing the ball, come into play. If you have the ball or your opponents have it, things are clear-cut. Its X's and O's. Just be in your position, applying the principles, and the only difference between the teams will be in technical execution. But the fact that the ball changes hands at inopportune and unplanned times creates a problem. The transition moments, winning and losing possession represent the time players need to shift between attacking and defending positions, roles and back again.

Unfortunately for them, the game doesn't stop and they cannot take up their perfect positions like they get to do in training. They may have to cover several yards or more to get to their new correct positions while the game keeps moving. If they don't see the situation coming, the transition, they'll make their decision late, and get off to a slow start. Sometimes the player sees the transition but is physically slow and arrives at the correct position too late. Or, just as they react to one change in possession, the ball changes hands again and they're caught in the no win ping-pong world of continually changing tasks.

In any case it's very rare that all of your players will be in their proper position at the same time. The game changes very fast and players think and move at different speeds. This makes it difficult for the team to retain its correct shape and for everyone to play effectively. For example, when the back players need to push up to support the midfielders some will move slowly, others quickly and you end up with a ragged line, with the gaps between players growing. It gets harder for the players to support each other and to play effectively.

Wait More Conflicts! Supplemental Tasks

All this gets more complicated for the team in possession because you add supplemental tasks — the secondary concerns that represent opportunities, the icing on the cake. For example, the basic offensive task for a midfielder is to support the top players from behind; whenever the top players get into trouble, midfielders should be in a position to receive a back pass and then play it forward. But midfielders could also have the supplemental task of moving ahead of the top player and into the space behind the opposing defense. The better the players, the more supplemental tasks they can handle.

The danger emerges when a player, usually a more talented one, forgets their basic tasks and concentrates on the supplemental ones. In this case, the midfielder might go forward in search of goals and never come back. Then, either the top player will be forced to take over the midfielder's job, or the two of them will be fighting each other for the same space, leaving the midfield vacant. Supplemental tasks will increase the potential for conflict, misunderstanding and miscommunication throughout the team. In the end, the basic tasks are responsibilities, and the supplemental tasks are opportunities. Always take care of the responsibilities first. (Make sure you can pay the mortgage before you buy the big screen.)

If every player's tasks could be built only around the principles of play your job would be a lot easier. The game would resemble the X's and O's on a chalkboard. "At this moment you're here, at that moment you're there." But soccer isn't static like that. It flows within the element of time. In that sense soccer is an event, existing in four moments and not static principles. Thinking in 'time terms,' i.e. the four main moments, is important to playing better soccer. It helps the coach have a more balanced point of view when observing the team and allows players time to switch gears and take up their new responsibilities. It's the wiggle room in the game clock.

The Soccer Cycle: Four Moments - Repeated

When a spectator watches a game, it has a flow from beginning to end. It's a seamless, linear event from the opening kick off to the final whistle. But for the players and coaches the game exists in four moments that repeat in the same order time after time. The only variable in the cycle is the amount of time a team will spend in any one of the moments.

The four main moments are built around ball possession, starting with who has it and who doesn't. For you and your players, this outlook translates into the two key moments: "We have the ball" and "They have the ball."

But in youth soccer, ball possession doesn't last very long. These two moments are constantly transitioning from one to the other. So the times when the ball changes hands become the other two main moments, the times when your team is in the process of either winning or losing the ball. (Some youth teams spend more time in the transition moments then they do in the possession ones!)

Looking at the game this way, you'll see the added element, transition. The principles of play, as we saw them in Chapter 3, don't contain the element of "time" for the players to move between having possession and the opponents having possession. They are a black and white, static view of the game.

The transition moments link the two sets of the principles of play in the real world. Children are very slow moving between the moments. When slow mental speed is combined with slow physical speed and rapid turnovers, it's no wonder that some children look like they're stuck in last week's game.

For example, when your team has a corner kick all of your players think in attacking, "we have possession terms." Everyone is involved in the attacking plan, from your strikers to your goalkeeper. But say the corner kick is a high, lazy floater that should be no trouble for the opposing goalkeeper. Now your players have a problem. Do they continue to think in attacking, "We have the ball terms" or do they start thinking in transition, "Uh-oh, this doesn't look good terms?" The decisions they make, based on the way they read the situation, are critical. He or she who thinks the fastest starts the quickest.

Then, the goalkeeper catches the ball. All of your players must now switch to "They have the ball" think and act accordingly. Like most youth goalkeepers this one runs to the top of the box and punts the ball towards midfield. The ball drifts lazily towards three of your defenders and one of their strikers. While the odds favor your team winning the ball 3:1, no one can be certain about the outcome. Half of your players start thinking, "We're going to get the ball," while other half thinks "still their ball." Each group bases their actions on these thoughts. Half of your team moves into attacking positions while the other half moves to defend against the new perceived threat. Because the team is playing to two different plans, they go their separate ways. This isn't good.

Eventually your team regains possession and the cycle starts all over again. This is how the entire game flows for the players. Having possession, losing possession, opponents in possession and regaining possession. Keep in mind how quickly this one scenario happened – just 10-12 seconds! – And draw it out over the course of the entire game. You'll begin to appreciate how much room for error runs through a match and the size of the problem. It also demonstrates how important small-sided games are. With their transition moments as a normal part of the game they include this element in player education. Drills that begin and end in specific moments fail address this issue.

Conclusion

As the players grow into the eleven-a-side game they should become more "job specific" and less "position bound." Players will gravitate naturally to a specific role, a ball winner, goal scorer or playmaker, one that closely suits their needs and abilities. Most likely this role won't be limited to a single position, i.e. central striker, but can be filled from several different ones on the field. By focusing on how they can contribute to the game, the tasks that they can fill, players are insuring that they bring more universal value to the team and aren't just limited to playing "right back." This is important in youth education as players move from team to team. It reduces the chance of a talented younger player being stuck on the bench because they are competing for a single position with an older established one. They can do the same job, just in a different place.

Chapter 5

Why goals are scored

After all of the talk about lines, principles, tasks and so on it's about time to take a look at what the game is really all about. Goals. Either scoring or stopping them.

There are five basic reasons why goals are scored. But one reason by itself usually doesn't result in a goal, or even a shot. Rather, it's when two or more happen simultaneously or in close succession that a goal-scoring chance is created.

1. **Failure to pressure the player with the ball**. Of course you want to pressurize attackers when they are within shooting range of your goal, but there are also other times when pressurizing the attackers is important.

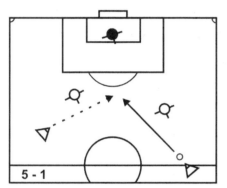

In diagram 5-1 the defender is too far from the attacker with the ball and is giving her too much space. Even though the attacker is in her half of the field she is still a threat and is able to deliver a deep pass to her teammate. In this case the defender should be between two and four yards away from the attacker. Close enough to limit her ability to play the deep pass but not so close that the attacker can easily dribble past her.

2. **Failure to provide cover for the pressurizing player**. Defenders are human and they are going to get beaten from time to time. An organized defense will have more players in the vital space then the attackers and the pressurizing player will have a free teammate close by to back them up in this event.

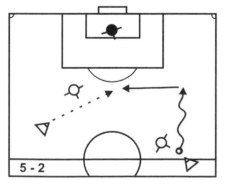

In diagram 5-2 the defender has moved into a good pressurizing position but the attacker has been able to beat her on the outside. Now the attacker has a free run into the penalty area because the second defender is too far away to be of any help. The first defender doesn't have any covering or supporting help nearby. If the attackers can create enough 1v1's eventually they'll win one or two. That might be all they need to win the game.

3. **Failure to track players down**. When attackers make aggressive runs, especially towards the back of the defense, they need to be tracked down right from the start. Too often a back player or midfielder will make a run forward and their immediate opponent just lets them go.

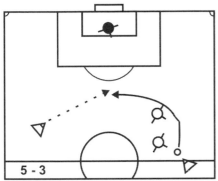

After the last attack, Diagram 5-2 the second defender has moved across to provide cover for the pressurizing player, Diagram 5-3. This time the attacker with the ball has been able to pass it into the space between the backs and the goalkeeper for the second attacker to run onto. In this case, there's no one marking this free attacker moving forward. When attackers get behind defenders it poses a real problem for the defense. When the defenders don't know the attackers are there it poses an even bigger one. (This qualifies as an example where there isn't effective pressure on the player with the ball and failure to track the player down.)

4. **Giving the ball away**. Whether it's a bad pass, poor control or losing the ball in a tackle giving the ball away can be 50% of the way to conceding a goal. When you keep possession of the ball they can't score.

Giving the ball away maybe the number one problem in youth soccer, it certainly ranks right up there. Only when a team develops a healthy respect for maintaining possession and can hold the ball for extended periods will they have a positive impact on the game. This allows the players the time necessary to read, plan and execute their actions. The irony of this is that, in youth soccer, it's often the coaches and parents who are the culprits in teaching children that ball possession isn't important, that giving the ball away is not just acceptable, but in some cases preferable. The following examples should help to illustrate this point.

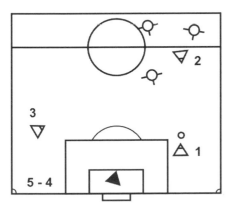

One piece of advice that you hear a lot from the sidelines is to "never pass the ball across the face of the goal, pass it outside." In Diagram 5-4, if attacker number 1 follows this advice his only target is attacker number 2. Passing there will likely end up in giving the ball to the opponents. Instead, the correct pass should be to attacker number 3, even if they have to go through the goalkeeper first. Be careful of setting up dogmatic rules which maybe at odds with a useful solution.

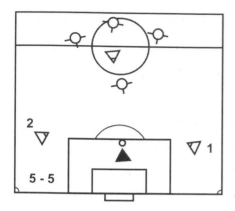

Diagram 5-5 shows a second situation seen all too often at youth games. The goalkeeper is in possession and punts the ball towards the center circle where four defenders are marking one attacker. The result is a battle and most likely loss of possession. This geographic solution, getting the ball as far away from your goal as possible, is at best short sighted. At worst it teaches the players that it's O.K. to give the ball to the other team. A better solution for the goalkeeper would be to roll or throw the ball out to either one of the back players, numbers 1 or 2, or simply put the ball on the ground and let the opponents come towards him. This will empty out the midfield and make it easier the top player to find the space he needs to get open. Building up out of the back is a valuable skill that is often ignored because coaches and parents are afraid of a mistake in the back third of the field. This fear is transferred to the players, creates a real problem in their mentality and increases their fear of failure.

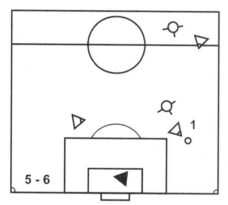

Diagram 5-6 shows another common situation. Attacker 1 has possession but is under some pressure and heading in the wrong direction. If the thinking and advice from the sidelines is "When in doubt kick it out" attacker 1 will be happy to give the opponents a throwin in the back third. Again, this reinforces the idea that ball possession is a secondary, even unimportant concern. Instead, the player should be encouraged to consider the problem and to try to find a solution that keeps possession of the ball. Giving the ball away is a last resort, especially in your own back third.

5. **Restarts**. Corners, free kicks, penalties and throw-ins offer an excellent chance to score. It's difficult, if not impossible to put pressure on the player taking the restart and with rehearsed runs attackers can get free from their defenders. They represent an opportunity for rehearsed attacking moves with an unpressured service.

You can make a career out of coaching just these five points both offensively and defensively. Simply watch a small-sided game and analyze why the goals were scored or not scored. Then help the players learn how to create and take advantage of the reasons when they're in possession and how to minimize the problems when they're not. And that's one of the nice things about small-sided games. They offer lots of goals so you'll have plenty of opportunities to coach on either side of the ball.

Chapter 6

Organization Starts With the Defense

Organizing the team's defensive duties is easier than organizing its attacking functions. First, defenders don't have supplemental tasks; they only need to be concerned with the most important basic task at the moment. Some coaches simplify these by restricting a player's freedom — telling a child to play on a specific spot or line; limiting a player's 'job' to defending the goal; telling kids to just kick the ball out of play when they're under pressure, and/or that they should never go ahead of the ball and join in the attack.

The problem is instructions like this paint a negative picture of the player's role in the game. They can help set up the party, but they're not invited to it.

Still, there's no question that defenders do the heavy lifting for the more glamorous attackers. Identifying players, especially talented players, who will accept and want to excel in the job will be difficult.

The bottom line is that the opportunity for fame and glory begins the moment that we lose the ball because until we get it back we're out of business. And individuals who can excel in this skill are worth their weight in gold.

Essentials: Goal Side, Sideways on, Distance and Angles

To win the ball back, the defender first should be on the goal side of the ball.

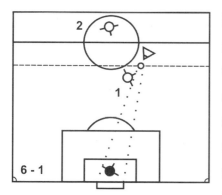

Diagram 6-1 shows two defenders, goalkeeper and one attacker. Defender number 1 is goal side of the attacker with the ball. He is on a line between the attacker and the goal, creating a problem the attacker will have to solve. Defender number 2 is not goal side of the ball and doesn't present any problem to the attacker. Defender number 2 has to decide if he should recover goal side, across the dotted line, or hold his position. If Defender number 1 can handle the situation he doesn't need to. That saves Defender 2 the run back. When the back players are effective defending in 1v1, the rest of the team can play more aggressively and it saves everyone a lot of energy.

But just being goal side isn't quite enough. The pressurizing defender also needs to be at the correct distance and angle from the attacker. Young players usually stand square to the attacker, literally toe-to-toe on parallel lines, with the defender's right foot across from the attacker's left and vice versa. This can cause additional problems for the defender.

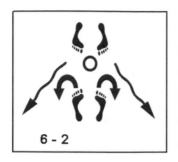

6 - 2

Diagram 6-2 illustrates this situation and the problems the defender faces. This position is called "being square" and gives the attacker these advantages: They can go around the defender on either side or play the ball between the defenders legs, the dreaded nutmeg. While the defender is already ahead of the attacker she will have to turn 180 degrees and that makes her a step slower. Add to this, the attacker controls the start. They get to say "Go" in the race between the two.

6 - 3

In Diagram 6-3, the defender is "sideways on" to the attacker — she's still ahead of them, still in the space the attacker wants to move into.

But now the attacker can't beat the defender going to her right, that way all she can do is go square across the field, and it's no longer possible to go between the defenders legs. If the attacker wants to dribble past the defender, the only option will be to go in front of her. Now the defender only needs to turn through 90 degrees at the most. This gives her a greater degree of control and limits the attacker's options to one, a big advantage to the defender.

Neither 6-2 nor 6-3 shows a static situation. The attacker will move forward, and try to dictate what will happen. The defender will try to slow the attacker, while her teammates organize to meet the threat. The defender will trade space for time, exercising self-control and restraint and the attacker will be looking for the right moment to either take her on or to call off the whole affair and pass the ball to a supporting player.

Sideways on offers the defender other benefits. It can take away one of the attacker's feet and if it's the attackers dominate foot it's another advantage to the defender.

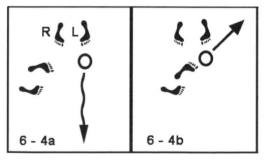

6 - 4a   6 - 4b

In Diagram 6-4a the attacker will try to keep the ball as far away as possible from the defender, and in doing so will be forced to favor her left foot. If the attacker's right-footed, this will add to their problems and help the defender.

If the ball gets ahead of the attacker, the defenders nearest foot might slide in for a toe-poke tackle (Diagram 6-4b). This can put the ball behind the attacker. With the defenders weight and momentum going in the direction of the ball, and the attacker's away from it, it's another advantage of being sideways on.

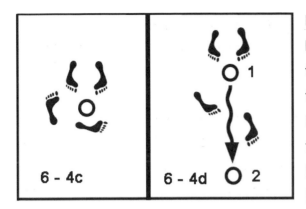

6 - 4c   6 - 4d

Diagram 6-4c shows the defender going in for a standard block tackle: From the sideways-on position, the foot closest to the ball steps up alongside, while the tackling foot, toe pointing towards the knee and the ankle locked, follows and blocks it in. The defender needs to strike quickly, decisively and drive through the ball. Bending the knees and trunk, the defender's body needs to be low and compact, with her weight distributed behind and slightly over the ball. Then defender can straighten up through the attacker and move into the space behind them.

The sideways-on position provides an answer when the attacker has committed to beating the defender with the old push-and-run. In Diagram 6-4d, the defender knows which side the attacker will use and is already slightly ahead of them. The defender only needs to step across the path of the ball, just after the attacker pushes it past them but before they can catch up to it themselves at position 2. The defender separates the attacker from the ball and steals it easily.

But don't stop yet! The defender, now an attacker, should immediately look for a supporting teammate, preferably one who can launch a counterattack, and avoid undoing a good defensive effort by making the mistake of turning back into their former attacker, who's now a defender.

Goal side and sideways on are just part of the battle. They won't matter if the defender is too near or too far away from the opponent. The defender also needs to be at the correct distance.

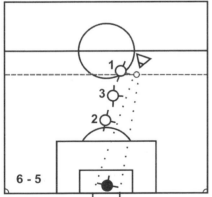

6 - 5

Diagram 6-5 shows three different defensive positions, each on the goal side of the attacker and sideways-on. Position 1 puts the defender too close to the attacker. They can get by the defender and be on the way to the goal with a single step. Skip down to Position 2, there's no pressure on the attacker and that means they can attack the defender at speed or pass at will. The defender is too far away.

That leaves one choice for the defender: Position 3. It's close enough to threaten the attacker and still far enough out — 6–9 feet —that they cannot simply run past the defender. This distance also makes it very difficult for attackers to make a long pass or take a shot, because they need to be far enough away from the ball to take a long stride into it. A distance between 6 and 9 feet gives the defender an excellent chance to win or block the ball while the attacker is taking that last long stride.

Showing the Attacker Inside or Outside & Preventing a Turn

Many youth coaches hold to the doctrine, "Always send the attackers outside or down the line." Let's take a look at the reasoning behind that idea and an alternative.

In Diagram 6-6, Defender 1 is showing the attacker down the line. The idea is to keep the attacker pinned between the defender and the line itself, limiting the attacker's useable space. The defender can jockey the attacker deep towards the corner flag until the correct moment to tackle. The basic idea is, the farther the attacker is from the center of the field, the better.

But there are some downsides to this. First, the attacker is also holding the defender outside. This stretches the defense across the field and makes it harder for other defenders to support the pressurizing player. (We'll see later on, defenders want to recover into the center keeping with the principle of concentration.) As the attacker moves down the line the defender follows them and moves farther away from teammates and support. Finally, the defender who can get in a tackle will usually be facing the sideline and have a very limited view of passing options.

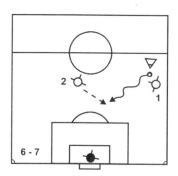

Diagram 6-7 shows an alternative. Defender 1 is showing the attacker inside, sending them into the most crowded space, the center of the field. As the attacker dribbles forward they're moving closer to the supporting defenders. As a result, the attacking team loses width, and the defending team gains a more concentrated defense. Also, if Defender 1 gets a tackle in here, they're facing into the center of the field and may have a better chance of launching a counterattack.

If the attacker beats the defender down the line in the Diagram 6-6, Defender 2 might have to cover 20 to 25 yards to reach the attacker. More space means more time, and this gives the attacker precious seconds to look up, assess the situation and take advantage of the lack of pressure. On the other hand, in Diagram 6-7, Defender 2 will need to cover a much shorter distance to pressure the attacker.

A secondary benefit of bringing attackers into the center of the field is that you have a good chance of forcing them to use their "bad" foot — the attackers on the right side are usually right-footed and on the left, well, sometimes they're left-footed. Forcing them onto their weak foot will limit your opponent's technical ability and lower the quality of service they can provide.

Several factors can influence where you want to send an attacker. You might choose to show the opponents into the center of the field only in their half and down the line in your own. You might want to keep a tricky, but slow, attacker isolated outside, and send a fast and direct attacker inside. Everyone on the team must understand and be in agreement; the decision will affect each player's basic task and the position they'll need to be in to execute it.

When you're pressurizing an opponent who's facing his or her own goal, the main objective is to prevent the player from turning with the ball. The best way to do this is to force the opponent back towards their goal, keeping the player off balance and their vision down on the ball.

An opponent whose vision is focused that way will take in less information for decisions, and it makes them that much less of a threat. In this case, you'll need to move in much closer than when you are facing each other, even within arm's reach of the attacker.

6 - 8

In Diagram 6-8, when the attacker has the ball at Position 1, the defender should get very close and slightly to one side. The defender will also need to bend the knees and trunk to see around the attacker or between their legs. Too often, defenders stand directly behind the attacker and too high, almost standing straight up, so they can't see the ball or control which way the attacker can turn.

You'll want to guide the attacker to one side and wait for the opportunity to tackle. When the attacker turns and puts the ball at Position 2, halfway through the turn, they'll be exposing the ball and this is the moment to strike. At this point, you'll need to focus all of your attention on the ball. But you do need to remember: Tackling from behind is dangerous and illegal. When in doubt, contain the opponent and wait for a better opportunity. Win the ball, don't give up the foul.

That accounts for three quarters of the battle. The last 25 percent is a simple mixture of courage and tenacity. Without these all of the positioning and jockeying won't matter. In any given game, the result can always come down to who wants it more and who is the quickest to grab the chance.

Recovery Runs and Lines

Here's another problem for the youth soccer players: They don't recover far or fast enough, especially on the flanks. The outside defenders may follow the attacker who has just beaten them rather than recovering towards the goal. (Remember, head 'em off at the pass!) They'll be close enough for a photo op, but not close enough to be of any use defending. Compounding the issue are the players on the opposite side of the field. They often fail to recognize that there even is a problem. The distance across the field seems to clear them of any responsibility, and they don't start running (recovery) until it's too late. (Attackers don't seem to be too bothered by this. They usually start running right away!)

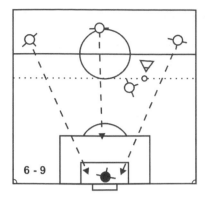

6-9

As you can see in Diagram 6-9, recovery lines resemble a funnel. The team needs to regroup, concentrating in goal-side positions. The players on the outside run towards their goal posts and players in the center run towards the penalty spot. As soon they are goal side of the ball, the dotted line, the players need to reevaluate the situation to find the best way to contribute to the team. They want to recover deep enough that they won't be quickly put out of the game again, but not so deep that they can't be a factor in the immediate defensive scheme.

Keys to Factors in Challenging for the Ball

A player who has committed to pressurizing and winning the ball needs to keep a few key concepts in mind.

Start Fast, Arrive Slow and Angle of Approach

The first thing that you want to do is to close down on the opponent while the ball is in flight. The attacker doesn't have control of the ball yet and you can safely close down the space between you and them. You want to get as close as you can while the ball is traveling so start early and start fast. If you can't get there in time for the interception look for the opportunity to tackle. If that's not there, slow down and just before the ball reaches the receiver get sideways-on and begin jockeying for position and control. Defenders coming in too quickly, too late or straight on set themselves up for trouble. An attacker only needs one touch to put the ball into the space behind you and your momentum will work against you. And by the way, you may have to make all of these decisions on the fly!

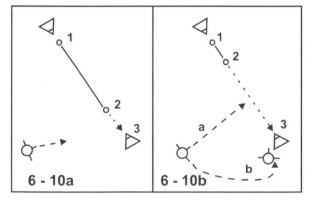

6 - 10a   6 - 10b

In Diagram 6-10a, the attacker has passed the ball and the defender started her run when the ball was at position 2. That only leaves her the time/space between points 2 and 3 to get into the correct position. The time/space between 1 and 2 is lost to her late decision. She will either arrive too late or won't be able to get close enough to pressurize the opponent.

In Diagram 6-10b, she has reacted sooner to the pass, starting her run when the ball was at position 2. There's more time/space between 2 and 3 then there is in Diagram 6-10a, (the ball needs to cover a longer distance.) This in turn, allows her to cover more ground to get to the best position. She has the option to intercept, line a, tackle or at least control the attacker, line b. When the defender chooses to intercept the pass they'll take the fastest route to the ball, a straight line as far from the receiver as they can get or as early in the balls line of flight as possible. When they decide to go in for a tackle or to control the attacker they'll bend their approach run slightly. Their first steps will be slightly off of the direct line to their target. This makes it easier to approach the attacker sideways-on. Going directly at them leaves the defender's approach square and gives the attacker the advantages that we saw earlier in Diagram 6-2.

In the two Diagrams, the difference is not in the players' speed of movement, but in the speed of reaction. In Diagram 6-10b the defender read the play, made a quicker decision and got a jump on the attackers. This quality improves as your players develop soccer insight. Players who read situations ahead of time appear quicker, because they think a step ahead of their teammates and opponents. Fast, decisive action leads to faster, more confident play.

Best of All: Intercept

The best course of action is for you to get to the ball before the attacker, essentially turning the tables and switching roles with them. This way they won't get even a touch, and will often be played immediately out of the game. For a successful interception, you need to anticipate the attacker's, both the passer and the receiver's intentions and beat them into the ball's line of flight.

Think Tackle

If an interception isn't possible, tackling is the next option. Below are a few situations in which you should consider an immediate tackle:

- **A free supporting player is in a good position and defenders outnumber attackers.** If that's the case, even if the tackle fails, a supporting teammate may be in a good position to win the ball.

- **The defender and ball arrive at the same time.** The attacker will need to concentrate on controlling the ball and the defender's presence may be enough to force a mistake.

- **A bad pass that gives the attacker problems.** The attacker's concentration may falter as they attempt to control an awkward pass.

- **When the attacker makes a mess of their control.** The ball bounces away from or gets stuck underneath the attacker. Punish the mistake before they have a chance to correct it.

- **The defender can totally dominate the attacker.** When the attacker is no match for the defender, don't let them into the game easily. Go out and take complete control of the situation.

A final note about tackling: Defenders, especially young ones, going in for a challenge must be very careful not to commit a foul. Children need time to learn how to control their own body before they can attempt to control an opponent's in a challenge. If they misinterpret your instructions and play recklessly, they can injure their opponents, themselves or both and that's not acceptable. That type of play is physically dangerous; it makes the game less enjoyable and in the long run, it will create a sour attitude toward soccer that can drive them out of the sport.

Stay on Your Feet

Defenders who go to ground reduce their team by one player. Consider it only as a last resort, a desperate measure for use in a desperate situation.

That said some player's will enjoy sliding to block their opponents. At first it can be an effective tactic, even fun for those who enjoy the physical contact and getting dirty. But as a tool to get to a higher level of play it isn't very useful. Often it's a sign that the player was in the wrong spot or reacted too late and now has to slide in desperation. Composure, concentration and being in control are more important long term. So always preach, stay on your feet!

Launch a Counterattack

The moment when you win the ball can present a golden opportunity for a counterattack. Your opponents may be too disorganized to stop a quick strike, their defenders spread out to support the now defunct attack. Several of their players may have even gone ahead of the ball which can put them on the wrong side of it. This leaves fewer defenders between you and their goal!

If that's the case, you need to recognize it, and act quickly. Any delay in the decision between launching the counter and building up the attack makes the former that much harder. Your opponents will use that time to reorganize themselves and the opportunity can be lost. Attacking speed of play starts with the question at the moment you win the ball, <u>is the counter on or off?</u>

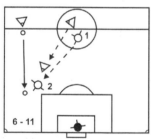

In Diagram 6-11, the attacker has passed the ball into the space behind the defender. The defender has recovered from Position 1 and won the ball at Position 2. However, the defender is facing their end line and the second attacker now has the defender under pressure. This is not a good position from which to launch a counterattack, and the new attackers team needs to recognize it. Instead, their first priority is simply to keep possession of the ball. Then the team can build up the attack to a more favorable situation.

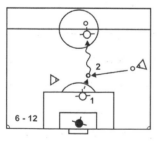

Diagram 6-12 shows a different scenario, an example of a good opportunity to launch a counterattack. The defender at position 1 has intercepted a pass at position 2. They are facing the opponent's goal with open space in front of them. The defenders, (now an attacker) first touch has put the two attackers, (now defenders) on the wrong side of the ball, they are in a poor position to do their basic defensive tasks. The defender can carry the ball himself or look to quickly pass it up field.

Don't Give the Ball Back

If the quick counterattack is not possible, the next most important objective is to keep the ball. Don't give it back to the other team by trying anything too brilliant. Defenders who have just come out of a tense 1v1 with the ball should quickly find a teammate who can receive it and make a composed decision what to do next.

If You Can't Win the Ball, Control the Situation

Finally, if you cannot arrive in time to intercept, and a clean tackle is not possible, you should try to control the attacker's options. Show them into to the least dangerous space, either inside or outside. Defenders in this situation will use self-restraint to buy time for their team to reorganize.

Team Pressurizing

There are two basic types of team pressurizing: high and low pressure. The first is used in the playmaking style and is marked by an aggressive, force-the-error approach. The second is more useful in counterattacking play where the defense is patient and restrained, more interested in guiding opponents into a mistake then forcing the issue. No matter which style of play you choose the following tips will help your team pressurize better as a unit:

- **Stay with the plan.** Before your team plays, they need to decide how they'll defend. How far up field the back players will go, the roles everyone will have when the opponents regain possession, how the lines will work with each other, etc. Without a plan it's every man for himself, a sure road to the "work harder, not smarter" school of soccer.

- **Players must push up together.** Goalkeepers who fail to close up with their back players, back players who fail to keep up with midfielders, and midfielders who fail to keep up with the top players allow big gaps to develop between the lines. (The exception would be in some counterattacking situations when the top players may have to strike on their own. The rest of the team stays behind and waits for the next assault by the opponents. While this creates a gap between the lines, it is built into the plan so everyone expects and is prepared to handle the situation.)

- **Top players must drop back.** The days of all glory and no work for forwards are long gone. The forwards represent the first line of defense as well as the last line of attack, and must work every bit as hard as their teammates to deny the opposition the chance to play.

- **The lines will have to shift across the field or into the center.** When the right back is busy marking the left winger then the left back needs to shift into the center of the field. When the center forward threatens the central defender the outside defenders will need to pinch in towards the center. (We covered this subject in detail in Chapter 3.)

- **Know when to retreat and when to stand your ground.** When a defender(s) face an equal or greater number of opponents, they should retreat to link with the next line of defenders.

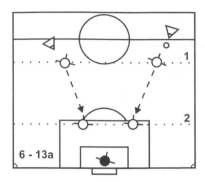

In Diagram 6-13a, two defenders face two attackers, i.e., a 2v2 at line 1. If the two defenders try to hold this line and lose, there will be a lot of open space behind them for the attackers to use. The best strategy would be for the defenders to retreat slowly to line 2. This will delay the attackers, give other defenders a chance to recover and bring the goalkeeper into the picture. The move reduces the space behind the defenders, slows the attack and changes the game to 2v3, defenders' advantage. Up to a point, defenders can trade space for time.

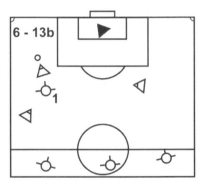

In Diagram 6-13b Defender 1 has the attacker with the ball facing their corner flag. This is a great opportunity for her teammates to press up and mark everyone close to the ball. Defender 1 doesn't even need to win the ball, just keep the attacker under pressure and don't let her turn. Her teammates should be able to pick up whatever pass the attacker tries to make to get out of trouble.

Support in Defense

Ideally defenders don't lose their 1v1's. But in this not-ideal world it happens, and teams must be able to deal with the problem the situation presents. The solution requires a free player supporting at the correct distance and angle, and they have to be there at the right moment.

The supporting player should be goal side of the pressurizing player; they have the responsibility of being the pressurizing player's eyes. The pressurizing player must focus complete attention on the attacker with the ball, so it's up to the supporting player to pass on information and make decisions. The supporting player will decide whether to send the attacker "down the line" or "show 'em inside." They can even see the correct moment for the tackle and offer encouragement. (This is not the time for coaches and parents to shout instructions from the sidelines — instructions and encouragement are the supporting player's job here, so don't help them.)

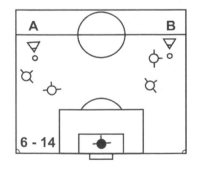

The defenders on the left side of Diagram 6-14A are in a good position to show the attacker inside. The pressurizing defender has taken away the outside and is showing the attacker directly into the supporting defender. The defenders on the right, 6-14B are showing the attacker down the line. Very often an attacker's vision and concentration is focused on the immediate opponent, they don't even see the second defender. The attacker will think there's space to run into, but the supporting defender can step in before the attacker has time for their first touch past the first defender. A good rule of thumb for the supporting player is to be 4 to 6 yards goal side of the pressurizing player. This should allow the supporting defender to get to the ball before the attacker.

If in doubt about the angle, players should take a 45-degree angle position from the pressurizing player. Being goal side allows them to react no matter which way the attacker moves.

Marking & Tracking Players Down

Individual defending includes marking players who don't have the ball. This can change the meaning to the term "goal side".

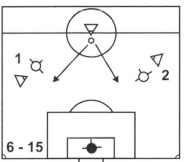

6 - 15

Defender 1 on the left side of Diagram 6-15 is goal side of the ball but not his immediate opponent. In fact the attacker is on defender 1's blind side. Defender 1 can see the ball or his opponent, but not both at the same time. When the attacker passes the ball into the space behind the defender 1, it will effectively put him out of the game. This is a poor defensive position.

On the right side, the defender 2 is goal side of the ball and his immediate opponent. From this position the defender can see the ball and his attacker at the same time. He'll be first to the ball if it's passed behind him and is also in a good position to intercept, tackle or contain the opponent if the ball is passed to their feet.

The difference in positioning is how you define "goal side." By using the ball as the reference point, as opposed to their immediate opponent, the defender on the left is technically in a good position. Remember, children will often take you literally. Earlier, when we looked at recovery lines, we said that players would first need to recover goal side of the ball and then reevaluate the situation. It's this reevaluation that can cause you problems. It leaves a lot of room for interpretation and will give you plenty of opportunities to help them to read these shades-of-gray situations.

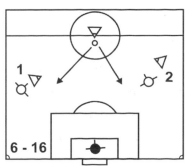

6 - 16

When marking players it's important to stay goal side/ball side. Defender 1 in Diagram 6-16 is on the corner flag side of their opponent. The defender can see the opponent and the ball at the same time, an improvement on Defender 1 in 6-15. But from this position they have little chance to intercept a pass towards the goal, the attacker is closer to the ball and goal.

Defender 2 is on the goal side and ball side of the attacker. They can see the opponent and the ball, and, like Defender 2 in 6-15, are in a good position to intercept, tackle or control the attacker.

Tracking players down means that defenders stay goal side/ball side of their immediate opponents as they move forward. Defenders cannot allow them to move into this space unmarked. We'll look at two moments when this is likely to happen.

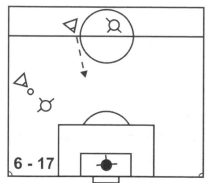

Diagram 6-17 shows an attacker following the play in late; the defender just let's the attacker go free and this creates a 2v1 for the attackers. Defenders who are ahead of the ball and track these runs immediately discourage opponents from moving forward. Attackers like to move into open space and when they see that the defender will come with them the space isn't open anymore. In fact, it can get very crowded. This can stop the run in the first few yards. Unfortunately, human nature often favors the attackers. They see the opportunity to go forward and join the attack; defenders (usually "attacking players" themselves) only see the responsibility of tracking back to defend. The attackers have a greater incentive, steal the first step and the defenders play catch up after that.

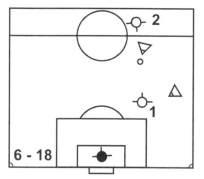

Diagram 6-18 shows the problem Defender 1 faces when the player ahead of them is beaten and they're already marking an opponent. If they move forward towards the attacker with ball their own opponent will be free in the space behind them. The best option in this case, facing a 1v2 is to retreat. They can trade space for time; link up with their goalkeeper and their teammates can recover goal side. By staying with their own opponent they eliminate the attacker's forward pass, the faster way to goal, leaving them only the option of dribbling forward. You must make the best of a bad situation.

Man-to-Man or Zonal Play

In their earliest years children should be exposed to a lot of man-to-man situations in small-sided games. This will require them to learn how to fend for themselves in the basic 1v1 encounters. Using a zonal defensive scheme is easy to organize but it has the down side of taking away some of the individual responsibility that children need to learn. When a teams back line contains players who are comfortable with man-to-man marking it allows other players greater freedom to go forward in the attack. When players aren't comfortable with these situations they can get nervous and this can spread through the entire team. Solid man-to-man play is the bedrock that all good teams build their defense on. Learning the skills young is every bit as important as learning attacking skills.

The Most Important Moment: When the Ball Changes Hands

All of this is well and good as long as you remember that your team's defensive organization comes out of your team's offensive organization. Players will need time to take up their new positions and tasks, to cover the space from where they were in those moments to where they need to be.

A key factor in helping the team in this critical moment is for the player closet to the opponent with the ball to apply pressure to him or her. They don't have to win the ball, if their presence causes the opponent to hesitate, to pass the ball square or backwards they have done their job. Winning the ball back is obviously the most desired goal. But if you can't do that then denying the opponent the quick counterattack is second. Buying time for the team to reorganize itself to meet its defensive tasks is a priority.

The clock begins ticking the moment your team loses possession. The slower your players start and execute the transition, the slower they'll play. Everything begins with recognizing the transition. Players who can see two or three plays ahead have a distinct advantage over those that can't. This isn't something that can be fixed in a single practice. It will have to be addressed time and again, and small-sided games offer the perfect vehicle to do it with.

> **Defending play is negative play. The sooner you end that phase the sooner you can begin the positive phases of Building Up and Attacking. The skills to do this must be used as a part of the everyday training.**

Chapter 7

Finish With the Attack

The chapter on defending examined some of the different ways a team can restrict the space and time available to their opponents. Now let's look at attacking play from the opposite perspective — creating space and time.

Stretch the Opponents

When you have the ball, your opponents will try to keep their team compact and limit the amount of space between and inside their lines. Defenders will funnel back along their recovery lines to gain a numerical advantage, Diagram 6-9. They want a concentrated block of players between you and their goal.

One of the first things that you can do to counter their efforts is to establish width in your attack. You stretch the defenders across the entire width of the field. This will open up space between the players in a line offsetting the other team's concentration-of-players tactic.

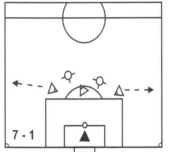

In Diagram 7-1, the goalkeeper has just caught the ball. The right and left back players move quickly outside, parallel to the end line. This is the fastest way for a team to develop width in its back and middle thirds. This gives the defenders the largest area to cover.

Often youth players are in too much of a hurry to get to the opponent's goal in situations like this. They move on the most direct line to the other goal. This is the same line that the defenders want to take. As a result, both opponents will be moving into the same space, at approximately the same speed. After running 20 yards there's no change in the distance between the attackers and the defenders. The attackers have failed to create any useable space. On the other hand, attackers who take the shortest route to the sideline will find open space within just a few yards, especially if their immediate opponent recovers back towards their goal. They are not running on the same lines. And if the defenders follow them "out wide" they'll become separated from their teammates. The attackers are creating useable space in the shortest amount of time.

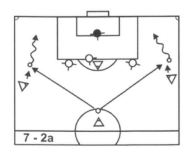

Diagram 7-2a shows how a three-player top line can stretch and pose problems for a concentrated defense. The defenders have retreated back to their goal, and the goalkeeper is acting as a sweeper behind them. They have built a solid block of defenders around their penalty area. If the attackers can switch the ball from the center midfielder to one of the wings they maybe able to penetrate around the back line into the space behind the defense.

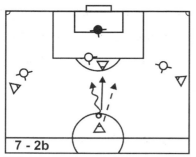

If the outside defenders counter this by closely marking the wingers, Diagram 7-2b, they leave the central defender isolated against the center forward. Now the midfielder can follow her pass to the center forward or simply carry the ball herself. Either situation creates a 2v1 in front of the goal.

When you're trying to stretch a team from end to end, you will either be spreading out the players in different lines or different players in the same line, e.g. the left back and left midfielder or the two central defenders.

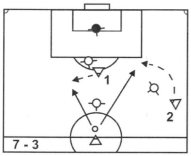

Diagram 7-3 shows attacker 1, between two defenders. (These could be the two central defenders, or they could be the center back and center midfielder.) The top defender is being drawn to the attacker with the ball, while the other is busy marking attacker 1. Attacker 1 is in the space behind, on the blind side of the pressurizing defender. By moving to her right, attacker 1 has become available for a pass in the space behind the pressurizing defender. The attackers have created space between the two defenders and exploited it.

Attacker 2 in Diagram 7-3 shows another way you can penetrate into the space behind the defense, this time using an overlapping run. The defender is ball watching and not paying attention to attacker 2. She can see the back of the defenders head and the ball at the same time. The defender has to split her vision between the ball and attacker 2, she never has all of the information she needs to do her job and this puts her under additional stress. (Blind side attackers don't call or shout for the ball, because that takes away the element of surprise.)

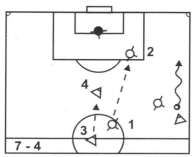

You can even create space by standing still. Diagram 7-4 shows the situation when the right wing has beaten her opponent and dribbled down the flank. In this case the central defender has to choose between two basic tasks: To stay goal side of the ball or to mark the center forward. The central defender decides to recover goal side of the ball, so she moves from point 1 to 2. But the center forward has only run from point 3 to point 4. She simply stopped and let the defender go on which opened up space between the two of them. The central defender is caught between conflicting tasks and the center forward has taken advantage of it.

Attacking Players With & Without the Ball

Defenders react or move in response to three things: the movement of the ball, the movement of opponents and or their teammates. Since the attackers control two out of the three they have an advantage in controlling where defenders will be. Creating space is largely a matter of either moving defenders out of good defensive positions into poor ones, or isolating them in a position they don't want to be in at all. Here are a few suggestions for getting defenders to cooperate with your attacking plans.

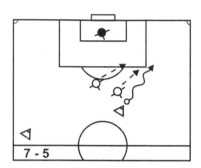

Diagrams 7-5 and 7-6 show what makes running with the ball such an effective way to move defenders into poor positions. In Diagram 7-5 the attacker dribbles towards the corner flag, and the defenders follow her. Both the pressurizing and covering defender are moving farther away from the goal. In this case the defenders are happy with the result, and so is the attacker.

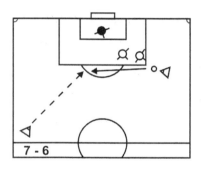

Diagram 7-6 shows the situation after the defenders followed the run outside. By using the ball as bait, the attackers pulled the two defenders into poor defensive positions. By running with the ball the first attacker opened up the center of the field for the second attacker to move forward into for a shot.

Overlap Runs Go Around to Get Behind a Line

We saw in Diagram 7-3 how attacker 2 was able to use an overlapping run to get behind her immediate opponent. Here we'll look at these runs in greater detail. Generally, an overlap is a run made by a player from behind and around the outside of another player. With its element of surprise, it's meant to get an attacker around a line and into the space behind it.

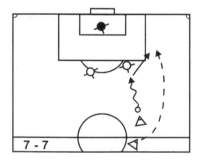

In Diagram 7-7 the attacker with the ball dribbles at speed straight at the defender. Defenders faced with this type of direct challenge often stand their ground, and as the attacker, that's just what you want. This can isolate and freeze defenders on the ground that you choose. The second attacker follows the first and times his run so that he can pass by the "frozen" defender into the space behind them.

Just before you enter the defender's tackling space, you pass the ball behind the defender so the overlapping player can run onto it. The pass must be at just the right moment. Too early and the defender can recover, too late and they can tackle.

By coming inside and directly at the defender, you will be able to hold the defense in place. In this case, the line won't shift over to meet the threat, because the threat, at least the one that they can see, is coming right at them. This creates more space outside for the overlapping player. If the defender moves into position to stop the pass outside, he'll be vulnerable to the dribble on the inside. (Note: It helps if the second attacker becomes the "eyes" for the first and talks to him as he commits to his run. The player with the ball's attention is focused on their immediate opponent and the overlapping player has a better view of the larger picture and can coach him.)

There are downsides to overlapping runs. One, when the defender wins the ball; neither attacker may be in position to do anything about it. It can leave you exposed to a counterattack. Second, midfielders who move past forwards are still midfielders, and the forwards who are holding in their place are still forwards. This affects the quality of the entire team. Players need to get back to where they belong as quickly as possible. Finally, they're hard work. For every 20-yard run forward, there's a 20-yard run to get back. This can produce tired players by the end of a close game. If the attackers can beat their individual opponents on their own then that's what they should do.

Decoy Runs

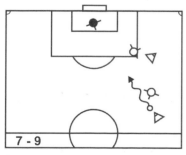

7 - 8

Sometimes players will make a run with no expectation of receiving the ball. The purpose of these decoy runs is to disrupt some part of the defenders' organization. In Diagram 7-8, the attacker is being pressured into the center of the field, and a covering defender is in a good position. The second attacker makes a strong run in front of the supporting defender and calls loudly for the ball. The second defender has to make a quick decision: Stay as a supporting player or track the attacker's run. In this example, the supporting defender chooses to follow the attacker.

7 - 9

Now the situation looks like Diagram 7-9: The decoy run has destroyed the defensive support, and the attacker with the ball, who faced a 1v2 a moment ago, now faces a 1v1. It's up to that attacker to decide what to do, whether to take on the defender or look for some other option. In this case the attacker chooses to take on the defender and dribbles inside, right through the space vacated by the supporting defender. (If the supporting defender decides not to follow the decoy run the second attacker may become a target herself.)

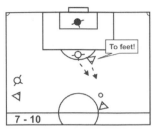

Players, especially top players, who only think of scoring themselves, limit their value to the team. As a prime target for close marking, top players can drag defenders around the field almost at will. They are a great source of decoy runs that create space and opportunities for their teammates. In Diagram 7-10, the center forward has called for and checked back towards the ball. The defender has followed her. (If the defender doesn't, the center forward can receive a pass, turn and then attack the central defender.)

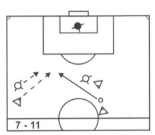

This creates the situation in Diagram 7-11. The center forward has pulled the defender away from the goal, creating space between the back line and the goalkeeper. The left wing runs into the space and receives the pass behind the central defender. The winger is moving from the outside, flank position, into the center of the field. This allows her to look across the field while moving forward. She can see the goal, ball and her opponent at the same time, an advantage over the center forward, who receives the ball with her back to the goal and opponent.

Decoy runs involve three players. The first is the passer. The second makes the decoy run and the third receives the pass. It involves an understanding and agreement to a plan the three create on the spur of the moment. They must communicate with each other quickly and execute the actions at just the right moment. 3v3 is a good form to introduce the idea of decoy runs and help players appreciate that sometimes they must sacrifice their own efforts so the team gains an advantage.

Checking In, Checking Out

Checking in and out, Diagrams 7-12 and 7-13, show how attacking players can create space for themselves. They're making their own decoy run by first moving away from the space they want to receive the ball in before they check back to it.

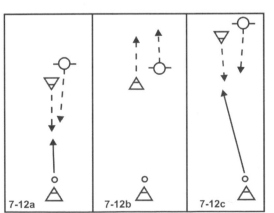

The attacker in Diagram 7-12a simply moves to meet the pass. This offers his teammate a good target, but the attackers can end up so close to each other that they don't advance the ball very far and an aggressive defender can put both players under pressure.

In Diagram 7-12b, the attacker first moves away from his teammate taking the defender with him. In Diagram 7-12c he turns and checks back, in, towards his teammate. The initial move away creates more space between the two attackers. If the defender lets him go then he can find a passing angle in the space behind the defender. At the least the two attackers are now farther apart and the net result is more space for a longer pass.

You can start this move slowly; a simple jog or trot may be all it takes to move the defender back. Remember, you don't want to lose the defender just yet. Then, when it's time to check back to the ball, move quickly. Even if the defender knows what you're up to, they don't know when you'll do it. The uncertainty is what makes checking back so effective.

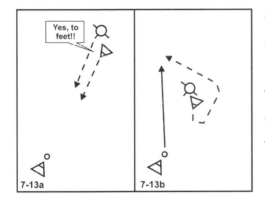

Checking out is a good way to create space behind you. First, there needs to be enough space already between the receiver and the passer like in Diagram 7-13a. This time the receiver moves quickly towards the player with the ball, calling loudly to convince the defender that a pass is coming. The objective is to have the defender follow and mark the receiver tightly; you want them to think "Interception."

As both players speed towards the passer, the attacker hits the brakes, turns behind the defender and moves back through the space they just vacated, Diagram 7-13b. The attacker can now collect a pass behind defender. Since the attacker chooses the moment to stop and turn they have the benefit of surprise, and the defenders own forward momentum should be enough to allow the attacker to get free.

For checking in and out to work, there must be very good understanding and communication between the passer and receiver. The passer must read the receiver's intentions to create the space and hold the ball, passing it at the correct moment. Pass too early, and the receiver may not see it or be in the correct position; pass too late, and the run dies. At the same time, the receiver has to time the run to work in conjunction with their teammate's situation. "Does he see me?" and "Will he be able to deliver the pass?" are just two of the questions the receiver has to consider before beginning his move.

Creating Space With Technique

Earlier we saw how running with the ball can create space by moving defenders, and how attacking a defender with the ball can freeze them in a poor position. Another dribbling technique used to create space is screening (a.k.a. "shielding") the ball. It comes into play when a player has the ball, is under a lot of pressure and has very little space to work in. With their vision focused down, the player's entire world will be limited to a few yards or even feet around the ball. Now the attacker will need to shield or screen the ball and look for help.

Young players caught in this situation need to know not to panic. Tell them, "If you're not sure where the defenders are, move where you know they're not." Too often young players get impatient, try to fight their way through the opponent(s) by turning into them and lose the ball. They need to stay composed and take advantage of what space they do have and keep possession until help arrives or they have the opportunity dribble out of trouble.

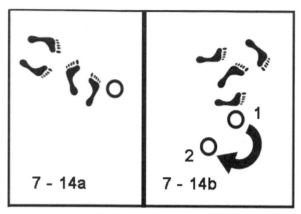

Diagram 7-14a shows the attacker screening the ball from the defender, keeping her body between the defender and the ball. By standing sideways on the attacker can see the defender and the ball at the same time. The attacker can easily roll, or push the ball away from the defender as they try to come around them, Diagram 7-14b. (Tell your players to use the outside of the foot farthest from the defender and not to turn their backs to them.) Defenders who become impatient may start to chase the ball and the attacker may be able to control them like a matador controls a bull.

Musts for Effective Crossovers: Timing & Communication

A player who's under pressure, along with a teammate might be able to get out of trouble using a crossover. This takes advantage of the defender's tight marking and concentration on the area just around the ball.

In a nutshell, crossovers are built on timing and communication. Both players must see each other, make eye contact and understand they are working together to solve the problem. Then, the instruction from the free player must come at the precise moment, not too early, not too late.

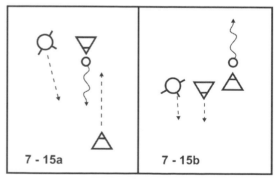

In Diagram 7-15a, the player with the ball is under pressure. She sees a teammate and begins dribbling towards her. Meanwhile, her teammate begins moving towards her, aiming to pass on the outside.

In Diagram 7-15b, the two attackers pass each other; the free attacker takes the ball and dribbles in the opposite direction while the first attacker continues on. The defender will be focused on the ball and never see the second attackers approach. The 180-degree change in direction can get the second attacker several yards past the defender in a matter of seconds.

The player without the ball is in control. She can see everything. She doesn't have to dribble or worry about avoiding a tackle — but does have the task of deciding if the cross over is on or off. This is determined by the position of the defender.

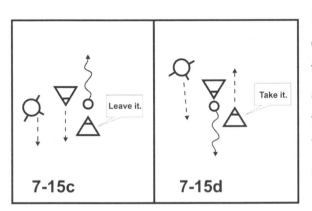

In Diagram 7-15c, the defender is slightly ahead of the dribbler, and the crossover is on. The second attacker sees the open space behind the dribbler. As the attackers approach each other, the second attacker decides to take the ball into that space and tells the dribbler to "Leave it." The dribbler leaves the ball and continues on her run as if she still had it.

7-15d shows the defender behind the dribbler, closing the space that the second attacker wants to move into, and the crossover is off. The second attacker says, "Take it," so the dribbler holds the ball and continues on her way.

Once the call is made, the dribbler must be careful not to interfere with the second attackers timing. She will expect to get the ball at a specific point and an extra touch by the dribbler can disrupt the whole thing. Additionally, the dribbler must carry the ball with the foot that is farthest away from the defender. The dribbler acts as a shield between the second attacker and the opponent.

Crossovers are effective even when the second attacker is marked.

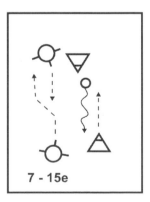

Diagram 7-15e shows what happens to two defenders when the attackers crossover. The defender marking the dribbler will be focused on her job, she'll be marking tightly and watching the ball. The second defender will be following the second attacker; she'll be able to see the dribbler and her teammate approaching. At the point where the attackers meet the second defender will have to detour around the crowd that she finds in front of her. This slight delay is all that the second attacker will need to escape her marker.

Creating Space with the Ball: Ball Control, Shooting, Passing

Good ball control is another ingredient in creating space, good players need less space to accomplish their jobs. But ball control is a means to accomplish other tasks. Whether it's a shot, dribble or pass the first touch should enable the attacker to move onto the next action.

Another way to create space: long range shooting. Players who can shoot from a long range can unlock a packed defense. Defenders cannot drop back into the penalty area and build a defensive block so close to the goal. They'll have to come forward and defend farther out than they might want, leaving space behind them which other attackers can exploit.

But quick, accurate passing is one of the best ways to create space because no player can outrun the ball. For teams to be able to play this type of "circulation football" all of the players will need a high level of technique, insight and communication skills. And you cannot depend on a few players to carry the load for the entire team. Inevitably, the ball will find its way to the weak link, and the system breaks down.

Teams can only play quickly for long periods when they are able to move and hold the ball on the ground. Taking the air route appears faster but results in players chasing after the ball, accompanied by an opponent or two. Also a ball in the air gives the receiving player added problems. They'll need to use at least one touch to bring the ball under control. When this happens, the receiver needs more space to control the ball, and will be under more pressure with fewer options available. The extra touch needed to control the ball has a negative effect on the players and teams speed of play. Children who move too early onto the big field and 11-a-side struggle with this, and the game often degrades into a battle to control geography through a never ending series of balls played "over the top."

Support Play Lives & Dies on Decisions

It would be nice to think that every time your team is in possession they could just go forward, score a goal and then reset for the opponent's kickoff. Unfortunately, this won't happen. Going forward often requires a detour, going sideways and even backwards. That's the consequence when the other team does its job, applying pressure and denying your direct route to the goal.

The first problem youth teams face in their support play is getting to the correct positions during the change in possession. The change begins as a team is in the process of winning the ball, not after they have already won it. Players need to move from tight, compact, (defensive) positions into more spread out ones. How quickly each player reads the change, begins moving and can cover the necessary ground are all factors in how quickly the team is able to build its structure for its build up and attack.

Add to this the typical reactions of youth players who win possession of the ball: "Get rid of it!" (i.e., the big boot/long ball), or "Score!" (i.e., immediately dribble toward the opponent's goal). In the former, teammates may not have had time to move into good positions and the ball immediately goes back to the opponents or out of play. In the latter, the player's head goes down, vision is lost and the attacker usually runs into trouble.

In summary, the first problem in support play occurs as your team wins possession. In a matter of seconds, the entire team must arrive at the same decision about the next step: Do we build up or launch the immediate counterattack? Only after answering this question can the players determine their correct positions, roles and opportunities.

Once players realize their team is regaining possession, each of them will need to consider what is the most important task they must perform — and it might be different than their basic or supplementary task. For example, when the left back and left midfielder have temporarily switched roles, and this particular transition requires the left back to continue playing in midfield and the midfielder to stay put in the back line. This was not in either player's job description at the start of the game, but it needs to be done — and done now. Players will have to think flexibly and meet the demands of the game as they arise.

As everyone begins to fill the basic tasks, some players will have to decide whether they should go ahead of the ball or not. If too few go forward, the attack dies; too many, and the team is vulnerable to a counterattack or the space up top becomes too crowded. Timing is another factor. Players who run too late or too early can cause more problems for their own team then they pose to the opponents.

Getting just the right balance of players behind and in front of the ball is a real challenge. But no matter how many players go forward or stay back the three key factors in how well a team supports the attacker are distance, angle and time.

Distance, Angle & Timing, Factors in Support Play

When players are supporting at an incorrect distance, two basic problems arise. When they're too close it's the dreaded bunch ball. When they're too far apart they can't reach each other. Either way, the team has a problem.

First we'll look at what happens when players behind the ball support from too far away, they can take the speed right out of the attack.

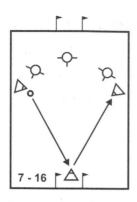

Diagrams 7-16 and 7-17 shows two 3v3 games with one major difference. In Diagram 7-16 an attacker is playing very deep behind his teammates. For him to receive and return a pass the ball has to travel a long distance. Remember, space equals time. The attackers speed of play will slow dramatically compared to Diagram 7-17, where the attacker has come much closer in support and the ball doesn't have to travel as far. In Diagram 7-17, the attackers can play quicker and give the defenders a bigger problem.

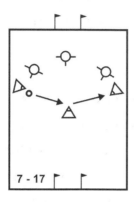

Furthermore, the deep attacker in Diagram 7-16 doesn't pose any threat to the defenders. If he were to carry the ball forward from such a deep position the defenders would be able to adjust and meet the challenge. But in Diagram 7-17 the central attacker is close enough to pose a direct threat to goal and could quickly attack any one of his opponents. To counter this the free defender will have to push forward and offer some resistance, allowing the outside attackers to play in a 1v1 if they get the ball.

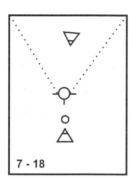

The biggest problem in the angle of support is that the ball should be able to see the receiver. In Diagram 7-18, the second attacker is standing in the defenders "shadow," inside the dotted lines. The only way the passer can reach her is to loft the ball over, or bend it around, the defender. Both options are difficult at best and provide more problems for both attackers.

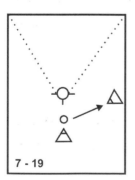

In Diagram 7-19, the receiver has moved out of the defender's "shadow," and into a space that's good for receiving a pass on the ground. The ball can "see" her. The passer can use her eye's to misdirect the defender, (Look left, pass right, or, look directly at, and freeze, the defender. This has the same effect as attacking with the ball.) The passer uses her peripheral vision to keep her teammate in view.

An additional concern related to the supporting angle comes when the supporting player is behind the ball. She wants to be at the correct distance and angle to receive the ball and also to be able to do what the player with the ball cannot do — pass it forward.

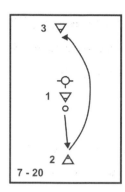

In Diagram 7-20 attacker 1 is being pressurized and cannot pass the ball forward to attacker 3. She has to look for help from attacker 2. In 7-20, attacker 2 is in a straight line with both teammates, leaving attacker 3 in the defender's shadow. To complete a pass to attacker 3, attacker 2 will have to either go over the top or around the two players in the middle. This is a more difficult pass for attacker 2 to make, and it will add to attacker 3's control problems.

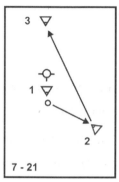

In Diagram 7-21, attacker 2 has moved to an angle that allows her to receive an easy pass and can now find attacker 3 with a direct pass on the ground. Everyone's job is simpler, and the team can complete this action much quicker and safer.

The final factor in good support play, timing, means that players must arrive at the correct position at the correct moment. Arriving in a good supporting position too early might attract a defender and take the supporting player out of the game. Too late, and the player never gets in the game. Supporting players need to learn the art of deception, checking in and out, looking away from the space they want to move into and how to work with their teammates to give the opponents as little information as possible.

Advantage Space

The passer is faced with two choices. He either passes the ball directly to the receiver's feet or passes it into a space where the receiver can move onto it. Passing to feet gives both players the easiest option. The passer has a real target to aim for, without the calculations that passing into space requires. A receiver who's positioned properly need only to move towards the ball to complete the pass. The downside of only passing to feet is that it can slow the team speed down and it lacks the element of surprise. It's basically only progressing from station to station.

Playing the ball into space requires a greater degree of communication between the passer and receiver. Both players have to read the either/or situations and arrive at the same decision in a split second, and usually without any discussion.

While passing the ball into space contributes to team speed, it can quickly get out of control. Young players may settle for simply kicking the ball away and sending their teammates off on a chase. The speed of the game quickly exceeds the abilities of the players. They end up working harder but not smarter. The best teams use a combination of playing to feet and to space. You play to feet to build up the attack, until the correct moment to pass into space arrives.

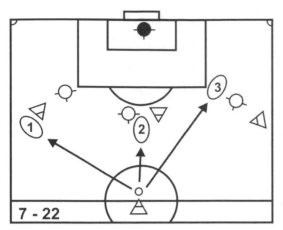

Diagram 7-22 illustrates the concept of advantage space. The space in Number one is the left wings advantage space. He should be first to any ball passed there. This is the safest route for the attackers.

In space Number two the ball is passed between the attacker and the defender. These "hospital balls" are rarely welcome for the receiver. A fight is almost certain and if the receiver is facing their own goal the defender will have the advantage of seeing the ball and both opponents at the same time.

Space Number three shows the attacker giving the ball away. He has played the ball into the defenders advantage space, that is, the defender should easily win 99.9% of every pass made here. Teams that accept this type of play, and there are a lot of them, are relying on hope. Hope that the defender will make a mistake and that they can capitalize on it. Hope that the top players can chase, harass and work hard enough, as defenders, to win the ball. But hope is a last resort, it isn't a plan. Youth players need to be encouraged to make better use of the ball then this.

These are just a few ideas for players to use when they want to create space in order to build up their play or launch an attack on the opponent's goal. It's the players who will have to decide all of the details of what to do in an actual match situation. What should be apparent though is that every one of the ideas can be introduced, developed and perfected using small-sided games. Games like 2v2 and 3v3 offer plenty of opportunities for children learn how, when and where to check in and out, run crossovers, overlaps, attack players with the ball, move opponents, blind side runs and so on. Achieving these small objectives is the focus of the training. Achieving them in match like conditions is the best training of all.

Barry Hulshoff:
"It was all about making space and coming into space. It is a kind of architecture on the field. It is about movement but it is still about space, about organizing space. you have to know why building up from the right side or from the left side is a different movement from when you build up from the center."
David Winner - Brilliant Orange, 2000, Bloomsbury Publishing

Chapter 8

Small-Sided Games Bring Technique Home

Sometimes, when coaches get together, the question comes up: What is more important, technique or tactics? Everyone weighs in with an opinion, and start choosing sides. Pretty soon, there appears to be two ideological camps, each sure the other is crazy or simply doesn't understand the question. That's because the real issue lies in the question itself, since the answer is "neither."

Technique without tactics is limited at best, as are tactics without technique. They're two sides of the same coin and you'll need to take that into account when you coach your players. Player education and development is about skill and that means using technique to solve a real soccer problem. That means TIC. It's not about mastering a technique for the sake of the technique. That's what physical education is for.

Technique can simply be thought of as the mechanics of how something gets done. While striking and receiving the ball, dribbling, heading and tackling all have very important mechanical points, too much emphasis on them can be boring and stifles a player's creativity. It can lead right back to the lines and lectures we got rid of in Chapter 1. In the words of the Positive Coaching Alliance such an overemphasis leads to "Draining the players Emotional Tank," a sure step to losing the their attention and concentration.

Players know they don't get points for style, and if they can get the job done, that just might be good enough for them. But when they have to take their game up a level, they may find those same abilities are inadequate. Now they have to find the motivation to focus on improving themselves.

Small-sided games provide an excellent tool to achieve this objective. Use games that require a higher level of technical expertise than the players currently have and their shortfalls will become apparent. Then, they can decide whether they want to invest the effort into any further improvement. Technique is only a means to an end, not an end in itself. If a player has reached what they see as their end, it will be difficult to persuade them that further effort is necessary.

Now we'll look at technique from the perspective of objectives and supply some very basic mechanics.

Passing with Value

Good passes are positive actions that contribute to the team; bad passes are negative actions taking away from the build up or the attack. In the list below, each action has been assigned a value. While you want your players to always look for the highest-value pass it has to be balanced by the risk to return. Many children think that they can hit a defense splitting pass every time — no matter where they are or what the situation is. This leads quickly to kick and run and loss of possession. Not good soccer. On the other hand, a player with the opportunity to play a penetrating pass but opts for one that just maintains possession has also played unskillfully. It's a lost opportunity. Developing patience in the build up and recognizing when to play the decisive pass is a vital skill to learn. One that is necessary as the precursor to scoring goals.

Type of Pass	Description	Value
Shot or goal	Think of shooting as passing the ball into the goal.	4
Assist	This pass leads directly to the shot.	3
Penetrating pass	By advancing the ball past a defender(s) or a line, this pass contributes to the build up and gets the team one step closer to an assist. Penetrating passes can be played from anywhere. For example: The goalkeeper rolls the ball out to the right back, who's behind the opponent's left wing. This pass puts the left wing on the wrong side of the ball and therefore out of the game. The greater the number of opponents put out of the game with a pass, the better.	2
A pass that keeps possession but doesn't put any opponents out of the game.	This pass contributes to the build up by keeping the ball away from the opponents. It represents at best a probe and at worst a safety first approach. While it's often played backwards or square it can be played forward in front of the opponents.	1
Crimes of Omission		
Missed opportunities	The team keeps possession, but has lost an opportunity. For example, a pass is played backwards, a 1, although a forward pass, a 2 is available. It takes take a degree of experience to see lost opportunities in the heat of a game — for coaches as well as players. New coaches tend to focus too much on the player with the ball, what's happening in their immediate space and their problems. Experience will help you to develop the necessary game awareness to see these missed opportunities.	0
Crimes of Commission	Crimes of commission are easier to spot, because the player has just given the ball to the opponents.	
A risk worth taking	Every player faces opportunities to try a difficult pass that could produce a good result. Encourage players to try when the risk is worth the return and to accept the consequences when they fail. It's important to have players who will take this responsibility. They aren't afraid to try the difficult; they can live with failure; and they are mature enough to calculate the chances of success and not just to rely on chance.	0
Giving the ball to the opponents unnecessarily	Sometimes it's because of a poor decision; other times it's poor execution. Either way, now the entire team must come together and work to correct the mistake. The difference between this error and the previous one is a matter of game maturity. This quality only comes through experience and that is best learned in small-sided games.	-1

Type of Pass	Description	Value
Giving the ball to the opponents is met with an immediate counterattack.	The team's lost possession and now faces serious consequences. Mistakes like this will largely take place in your own back or middle third.	-2

Just use the above as a general guide for yourself; it won't mean anything to your players if you tell them they hit a 1 or a –1. You can utilize small-sided games to analyze your players and use the information to guide your decisions and evaluations. For example, a player who consistently plays -1 passes is a poor choice for a key midfield distribution role.

Tips to Make Passing Pay

There are a few general rules that all players can follow that will improve the passing game.

- **Don't overestimate your own ability:** Too often players try to hit a game-winning, defense-splitting pass every time they get the ball. Relax, keep your composure and if you can't find a "good" pass quickly, settle for a safe one. The time that you're thinking about things is time a teammate in another position could make good use of the ball.

- **Always look for the deep pass first:** Look at the players who are at the edge of your passing range, and if you cannot get the ball to one of them, start working your way back. Make the first deep pass that <u>you can make</u>, and try to get as many opponents on the wrong side of the ball as quickly as possible.

- **Learn how to calculate the risk to return of each pass:** There are times to try the risky passes and times to play it safe. When in doubt, don't lose the ball, play it safe. Pass with a purpose and not just hope.

- **Don't telegraph your passes:** Look away from your target and use your peripheral vision. Your eyes can tell the defenders everything they want to know, so use them to misdirect the defenders.

- **Remember your teammate.** Keep in mind their situation, and what they need. If you can't supply them with the quality serve they require you should look for another target. Make them look like a better player.

- **Quick, simple and accurate passes get the job done.** Don't hold the ball and dwell over things. This slows down the team.

- **Don't run with the ball if you can't keep your head up.** Trying to run with the ball half the length of the field doesn't help if all you can see is the ball and your own two feet. Develop your field vision. And remember, the ball can travel faster without you attached to it.

Mechanics of Striking the Ball

Whether you're passing, heading or shooting, you're striking the ball. And just like any other sport where you do this — e.g., golf, tennis, baseball, even handball — your three primary mechanical concerns will be the approach, contact and follow-through.

Approach: From the Decision to the Moment of Contact

The approach is the time between when the decision is made to strike the ball and the moment of contact. The player will either move to the ball, the ball will move to them or both. This can be complicated if the player is under pressure from an opponent or if he or she delays their decision.

Angle and Distance

The correct angle and distance of the approach will depend on what surface you want to use, where you want to direct the ball and where the ball is when you make contact. The farther you want to play the ball, the longer your approach will need to be. The surface you want to use, the direction of the target and placement of the ball will determine the correct angle of the approach. For example, the approach for a push pass is along a straight line between the kicking foot, the ball and the target while a lofted instep pass will be around 45 degrees.

When you introduce children to kicking, you're going to see some of them stand with their non-kicking foot next to the ball, then swing the other leg to kick it. There is no approach at all, only the swing of the kicking leg. They need to open up their legs, stride into the ball in one smooth motion. The kicking leg does not draw back; rather, it follows the lead of the last long stride made by the plant leg.

The Plant Foot

As a general rule, the toe of the plant foot should be alongside the midline of the ball and pointing towards the target. The body must be balanced with the plant foot at a comfortable distance from the ball. Too close and you get jammed, too far and you have to reach for it. (However, if you want to lift the ball, the plant foot should be slightly behind it. This will help the kicking foot meet the ball below the horizontal line.)

Contact

This is the art of placing two square inches of body onto two square inches of the ball at exactly the right moment. It gets even harder when the ball is in motion, on a bad field and/or an opponent is trying to interfere. If there's any miscalculation in the approach, or an improper plant, correct contact will be difficult if not impossible.

Striking the ball, shooting, passing and heading produces a predictable, easily identified reaction. You can analyze a lot about the technique just by watching the flight of the ball.

Think of the ball as being divided along a horizontal and vertical axis. Strike it below the horizontal axis, in the O, it will rise; strike on the horizontal line, it will travel straight; above the line, it will go down. Contact on either side of the vertical axis, and it will spin in the opposite direction. On the right side, the X, will bend or hook the ball to the left and vice versa. To keep the ball level and straight contact must be made at, or slightly above the intersection of the horizontal and vertical axis.

Children who are just developing their ability to strike the ball benefit greatly from knowing specifically where to aim on the ball. For example, when you teach players how to kick a ball on a straight line in the air, they need to make contact at a very specific point (just below the midline and in the center, O in the Diagram above.) Contact anywhere outside this small space will not produce the desired result. At practice, find a panel on the ball that stands out, such as one with a logo or writing. Put that panel on the midline and then lower it to give the child a very specific spot to focus on. You can use this "magic panel" to set up the correct contact point on any dead ball.

Follow-Through

This is a huge problem for many children whose follow through often ends in crossed legs or a stab at the ball. View the follow through as the completion of a very smooth process. Whether heading or kicking, the player must play all the way through the ball not just at the ball. (Ask yourself this: After they have played the ball, are they free to continue moving, or have they come to a complete stop at the point of contact?)

Mechanics of Heading

The key elements in striking the ball, approach, contact and follow through apply to heading. The plant foot isn't such a big problem because by rotating the trunk and neck you can compensate for most problems. There are a few specific points that can help you coach this skill.

- **Eyes open, mouth closed, chin in.** Keep the eyes open, for obvious reasons. Keep the mouth shut so that the jaw provides a solid platform for the head.

- **Throw your eyes at the ball.** Attack the ball. Play it, don't let it play you.

- **Contact the ball with the center of the forehead.**

- **Look to your target.** Just after you make contact with the ball turn your head so that you can see where you want the ball to go. Guide the ball with your eyes. This provides the direction to your header.

- **Use a whip like motion from the trunk to generate power.**

Receiving & Ball Control

When receiving the ball, your most important task is to set up your next action. This means knowing what you want to do before the ball arrives. Without an objective already in mind, there really isn't any way to judge the quality of the control. "Oh, I meant to do that" can be the universal answer, or cop out to any result.

When you accept that "good ball control enables the next action," you create a certain standard for your training. An action must follow once the player gains control and they'll need to make their decision while the ball is in flight. As a coach, you cannot simply pass the ball to a player, watch them control it, and dub it "good" or "bad." This is going back to the P.E. model and the feedback is irrelevant. The quality of the controlling touch has to be seen within the context of the following action.

In setting this expectation, you create another feedback loop for the players. They'll know without you telling them if their control was poor, when it costs them the opportunity for a shot or the killer pass. Likewise, a player will see clearly, when a brilliant piece of control gets them, and the team, out of trouble or brings big rewards. Your players will learn from the game, without you as an external source for validation.

Mechanics of Receiving

There are two methods for controlling the ball, wedge and cushion control. Using the wedge method means controlling the ball between the body and the ground, usually with the foot and after a short bounce. Using the cushion method means using a body surface directly to control the ball. In either case the following represents the basic mechanics of ball control.

- **Get into the line of flight of the ball:** You can't control a ball if you watch it go by. Young children often run alongside the ball and fail to actually get in its line of flight.

- **Choose the controlling surface and present it to the ball:** While you're moving to the ball, or it's coming to you, you must decide which body part you'll use to cushion the ball. Failure in this step results in the dreaded "brain lock" and some fascinating physical contortions.

- **Present, relax and withdraw the controlling surface:** Think of "catching an egg," not bracing for a collision. A good baseball centerfielder uses "soft hands" to cushion a long fly ball. Soccer players follow the same formula, track, move to it, present the surface, relax and withdraw. Great players only need to move the controlling surface a minimal distance. They use good timing in place of greater movement.

Tips to Make Receiving Work

- **Show the passer an easy target:** Don't get lost in the defenders "shadow." Stay on your toes and constantly adjust your position to meet the changing needs of the player with the ball.

- **Move to meet the pass:** Attackers far too often wait for the ball to get to them and this is especially true when they are ahead of the ball. They want to continue in the direction the ball is traveling, so it's counterintuitive to move away from that space, back towards the ball. It seems logical to wait for the pass. Unfortunately, defenders usually don't oblige; instead, they move in for easy interceptions.

- **Moving to the ball also decreases the distance it has to travel, and therefore the time the ball is in flight:** That's the time you don't have control of it. Getting to the ball sooner means more time to execute your action so your team can play quicker.

- **Create space for yourself by first moving away from where you want to receive the ball:** Even a few steps in the opposite direction can get defenders to move and buy some extra space to receive the ball in. (See section about checking in and out.)

- **Choose the correct moment to move** A receiver who moves too soon will either have to stop and wait, killing the space and losing initiative, or keep moving past the space where they want to receive the ball. Moving too late means the defender can intercept the pass. Receivers must be able to read what the player on the ball is capable of and needs. They must work together; their timing and ideas must match.

Objectives of Dribbling

Dribbling just for the sake of dribbling does little to help the team. In fact, while the player on the ball goes through all six of his favorite fakes, the attack can slow to a crawl. Teammates soon learn not to bother moving to support players who only indulge themselves, which leaves the offending dribbler without anyone to pass to when the tricks have run out.

The bottom line: Dribbling, like every other action in the game must serve a purpose. Skillfully used, it will accomplish one of four objectives.

- **Move the ball into open space:** There are times in a match when the player with the ball needs to get into or through an open space. For example, the player who wins the ball in a crowd needs to get out of the crowd. Or, if there's no available target and 20 open yards, the player can run with the ball into that space, then reevaluate the situation.

- **Move the defender out of a good defensive position:** Here's the most common example: The attacker dribbles away from the space the ball needs to be in. If the defenders follow him, the run has opened up that space.

- **Freeze an opponent in a poor defensive position:** For example, before a defender can retreat to the penalty area a forward runs with the ball directly at him. In doing so, the attacker is challenging the defender to a duel and is choosing where it will take place.

- **Buy time:** For an attacker under pressure the most important thing is not to lose the ball. Attackers in this situation need to use their bodies to shield, or screen, the ball until help is available.

Children need to learn why and when to dribble as well as how. Helping them understand these basic objectives, and how they can use their own natural talents to achieve them, is a big step in helping them master this facet of the game.

Mechanics of Dribbling

Many different forms of small-sided games give your players the chance to master the mechanical components of successful dribbling. These are:

- **Close control:** "Close" is relative to the situation. If it's a breakaway in midfield, "close" might mean a distance of 4 to 6 yards; inside a crowded penalty area it could mean just 6 to 8 inches.

- **Change of direction:** Right then left, left then right, forward then back. A change in direction can move an opponent or the entire defense and open up space for the dribbler or a teammate.

- **Change of pace:** Slow to fast, fast to slow or even stop. Varying the pace produces the same result as a change in direction — problems for the defenders.

- **Disguise:** "Disguise" often refers to all of the moves that are designed to beat a defender, but it can also be something as simple as looking away from where you want to go. You can use those lying eye's!

For the majority of players the single most important trick is to disguise whether they will dribble or pass the ball. Selling the pass, then dribbling (or vice versa) puts the defender in a very bad situation. This skill can be easily taught in small-sided games that use the player's choice restart. Each restart sets up the confrontational moment and allows children to work on their moves and this particular skill in a real game.

Objectives of Defending

This topic has had it's own Chapter. However, a quick recap. When the opponents win the ball the closest players' objective is to immediately win the ball back, force the opponents to play predictably and finally to protect the goal, i.e. recover to a better position.

Mechanics of Defending

In addition to the key points in the chapter on defending, teach your players to stay low, balanced and on their toes. The fate of the game could hinge on the battle at their feet. Also, time favors the defense. Teach them to trade space for time until other players can come to the rescue and to be patient.

Finally, and this has been said before, whenever you win the ball, that moment presents a golden opportunity; if it's on, immediately launch a counterattack. The opponents are usually spread out supporting the attack and several may have moved ahead of the ball. Their defensive organization may be in no position to stop a quick strike.

Four Ways to Measure Technical Improvement

At the end of the session or season you'll want some way to evaluate how much the players have improved. While we'll look at evaluations in the Chapter on Coaching, the following can provide you with some useful, and general guidelines on evaluating technique.

- **Range:** Changes in the space or time of a technique affect the options available to a player. For example, a player who can pass the ball 30 yards has more options than one who can pass 15 yards. Reduced distance for ball control is another example; players with very close control will have more opportunities in a crowded penalty area than those who need more space. In a nutshell, these players can affect the game over a larger area and/or they need less space/time in which to work.

- **Scope:** As players develop, they widen their scope of play — i.e., the number of options available to them in a given technical area. The player who has learned to pass with either foot, or has learned to use the outside and the inside of one foot, has greater scope in passing than the player who can only use the inside of one foot.

- **Precision:** As their range develops, your players need to fine-tune it with a greater degree of accuracy. Being able to hit either of the receiver's feet at 30 yards allows a player to attack smaller spaces than one who can only hit the receiver's advantage space. The higher the level, the more precise actions are required.

- **Economy:** The better they are, the easier they make it look. Good players play with confidence and little wasted effort or energy. The fewer touches that can get the job done, the simpler the action, the more energy you save and the faster you can play.

As players develop the range, scope, precision and economy of their techniques, they gain greater control of their speed of play. Improvement in the four areas above makes technical execution almost instinctive. This frees up the mind to concentrate on creating and solving more complicated problems. This puts additional demands on them for new and even more improved technique, even higher standards.

All of these improvements must be viewed in the context of the game. Hitting a ball back and forth over longer distances, mastering a dozen fakes in the back yard, doesn't mean anything if its not transferred to the competitive match. Skill, the application of technique to solve a problem, can best be learned in small-sided games. Without the match as a guide your evaluation of the player's technical qualities will be limited at best.

> **Without doubt proper technique is vital to a players growth and development. But technique must be learned in the context of the match. It has to be applied to a problem and able to stand up under competition.**

Chapter 9

Not Just the Coach: The Soccer Doctor

Whether it's during a match or at practice coaching is a lot closer to being a doctor than you might think. Both start with diagnosing a patient; they require a prescription to treat a condition and finally adjusting that prescription to meet the changes that inevitably take place. Whether the patient is a single player, a line or the entire team the process is the same, observe, diagnose, prescribe and treat. To aid them, Doctors follow a set course of procedures that helps simplify their job. Luckily, you also have a procedure to follow and this Chapter will take you step by step through the process.

The Diagnosis – Reading the Game

To begin an accurate diagnosis you have watch the kids play soccer. Observing them do drills, juggle the ball, fitness tests — anything other than soccer — won't tell you very much about their real talents or problems. The match is always at the heart of the matter, and the diagnosis needs to begin there.

The examination should follow a logical series of steps, starting with the most basic concerns, than moving on to more specific ones. This requires a form of soccer triage to get quickly at the most important problem facing your patient. Set up a game and give them enough time to get use to it, the teams and conditions. Then compare where they actually are vs. where you think they should be. The gap between these points shows you the size of the problem.

Simplify Things

Still, even small-sided games can be pretty complex. You can simplify these games by eliminating nonessential variables. Your first step is to decide which team is having the biggest problem and focus on them. (After all, the other team by comparison is doing all right!) By eliminating one team from the picture you get rid of half of the problems right there! Then ask these six questions about the team you're watching.

1. **What moment contains the problem?** Because you're concentrating on only one team, this step narrows the diagnosis even more. By focusing on one team in one moment, you can concentrate on what is really important and disregard everything else. For example, the team you're watching is not generating any type of consistent attack. Now, you've reduced the diagnosis to one team when they are in possession. For the time being you can ignore what is going on when they are defending and the other team altogether.

2. **What is the problem?** This broad question is meant only to frame the team's general problem in that one moment. In this case, you notice that the players are getting caught in possession, they're holding onto the ball too long and their speed of play is too slow. The result, they don't have enough time to develop any attacking shape or ideas.

3. **Whose problem is it?** It's surprising how many teams have players named "someone," "everyone," "no one" or "anyone." You'll need to be specific and name names in this step — you

won't be able to fix anything until you do. Assign responsibility for the problem. In our example the left back, Sarah, keeps getting caught with the ball and giving it back to the opponents. So you focus on Sarah and what is going on around her when the team has possession.

4. **Where does the problem occur on the field?** Think in terms of the thirds of the field. For the example, Sarah only has the problem in her back third; she doesn't have it anywhere else, so the answer to where is in the teams back third, on the left side. The answer helps you to frame the field and goals for the next training session.

5. **When does the problem occur?** What event or situation triggers the problem for Sarah? Analyze what specific situation gives her so much trouble when she has possession in the back third. Continuing with the example, you notice that Sarah cannot find any targets to play the ball to. She either has to try to dribble out of trouble, ending up in a tackle or turns the ball over with a poor pass.

6. **Why does the problem occur?** The answer to this will be found in the shortcomings of Sarah's and her teammates TIC. (We look at TIC later in this Chapter.) Just ask yourself "What is going wrong for Sarah?" Is it a technical problem? Does she use too many touches and give the opponents a chance to steal the ball back? Is it a question of insight? Do Sarah and her teammates read the situation quickly and correctly? Is the problem in the communication between Sarah and her teammates? Does Sarah make effective use of her teammates and do her teammates offer her help quickly enough? Do they work well together? The answers will be important in deciding what coaching points you'll want to make and for fixing what ails the team. In our example, Sarah, Betsy and Karen are not playing together as a unit. Sarah's problem really belongs to the group and you'll have to address all of them together.

Soccer Problem Worksheet				
What moment is in question?	_Own team in possession._	Opponents in possession.	Change of possession, winning possession.	Change of possession, losing possession.
What is the problem?	_What are we doing/not doing? Unable to build up the attack. Giving the ball away too early and unnecessarily._		What are the opponents doing /not doing?	
Who is responsible?	_Who has to deal with this problem? Sarah - left back, Betsy - left mid, Karen – Center back_			
Where does the problem take place?	Attacking third.	Middle third.	_Defensive third. The left side._	
When does the problem occur?	_What event triggers the problem? When the left side gets possession in the back third._			
Why does the problem happen?	_Where is the breakdown in TIC? Betsy the left midfielder and Karen the center back do not offer support quickly enough. Sarah gets pressurized, caught in possession by the right wing. Poor communication._			

Diagram 9-1 shows a worksheet and how to progress methodically through the six questions. You can use the diagrams to fill in examples of the problem and help organize your thoughts. They also help by providing you with a "rough sketch" of what your training session will look like. Who will be involved, where and what goals you'll use. See appendix A for a blank form.

Correctly diagnosing the problem is vital in the preparation of a practice or for your halftime and post-game talks. This method will allow you to quickly arrive at a useful analysis of the situation, and help to avoid vague generalities like "We need to hustle more," "We need to pass better," "We need to take more shots," and so on. That information is so wide-ranging that it's irrelevant; it applies to no one and everyone, and it's doubtful that either is on your roster.

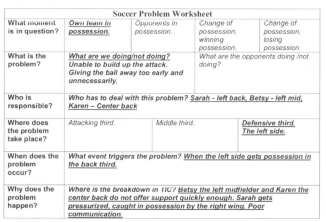
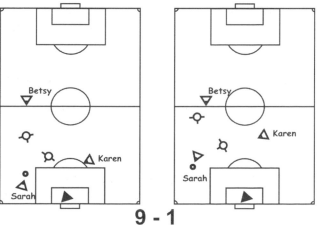

9 - 1

This method works well because it reduces the number of problems to something manageable. Rather than looking at the game and trying to itemize every crisis out there, you focus on identifying and isolating the single most pressing need. You can get your arms around a real concern and then concentrate on fixing it. The result is that you are left with the most practical information to help the team play better soccer.

The final benefit of this system occurs when your players begin to understand and use it themselves. When your team leaders are able to rapidly answer the questions they'll be able to solve the problems the opponents present while giving them harder ones to solve. You're creating your own coaching staff on the field.

When you start using this method, begin with games like 2v2, 3v3 and 4v4. They offer the simplest pictures for observation. Because the situations are straightforward, you'll quickly see who has the problem, where they have it and why. After awhile the steps will become natural for you and you'll be able to quickly analyze even larger games.

The Rx – Building a Game

After you've diagnosed your team's problem you'll need to come up with a solution, something that you can use to begin treating the soccer malady. The following steps will help you create a game out of your diagnosis.

- **Start with the players that have the specific problem.** Look at who is involved; it will give you the information you require to set up the teams. For our example, you'll need the left back Sarah, a goalkeeper, the center back Karen, the left midfielder Betsey and some opponents to work against. The number you choose represents the resistance that Sarah & Co. will have to work against. You can allow Sarah's team to have a numerical advantage until they get through the orientation phase of the game.

- **Create a field where the problem takes place.** Determine the type of field, the layout, dimensions, and the goals. (Think thirds.) Because this problem occurs in the teams back third, the big goal, the two small goals game is an appropriate place to start, see Chapter 11. Now you have the players in the correct area of the field and both teams have realistic objectives to play for, i.e. their goals.

- **Duplicate the event or situation that triggers the problem.** This problem exists for Sarah & Co. when they're in possession. You'll need to make sure that they get to handle the ball a lot and you can do that by controlling the restart. By having the goal keeper restart the game with a new ball in every time the ball goes out of play, Sarah's team will have many opportunities to build up the attack in the back third.

- **Include only rules that can aid in the lesson.** Avoid rules like offsides, kick offs, corner kicks or throw-ins that can slow the game down and/or don't help with what you're trying to get across. They're just a distraction and take you farther away from the learning/coaching moments that you're trying to create. Diagram 9-2 shows a form that will help you organize a session. In the top, put your basic information. This will help you stay on topic. In the first column, basic organization, outline each activity, note the layout, dimensions and equipment that you might need. In the middle column, action/rules/progressions, note any developments or changes that you might want to make. In the last column, coaching points, list the basic ideas that you want to get across during each part of the session. Keep it short and simple. See appendix B for a blank form.

Training for: HotShots U-12 Girls	Location: Hyland Center	Date: 9/24
Analysis of problem: Poor build up out of the back.		
Objectives for the session: Improve communication and understanding between backs & midfield		
Main moment: Own team in possession Field third: Back third		No. Of players: 16
Basic organization:	Action/rules/progressions:	Coaching points:
Warm up 3v2 - Line soccer/goal 12x20 yds	* 3 play line soccer * 2 shoot to goal * Rotate players	* Coach the three * Build up, don't hurry * Find the open player * Don't lose the ball
Big goal/2 small goals 38x20 4+GK vs. 3 Three team rotation	* 5 players score in small goals * 3 score in big goal. * Rotate teams every 4 minutes * Increase defenders as needed * All restarts from the GK to the team going out * Keep extra balls in the goal	* Get into position to receive the ball every restart * Work together, find the open player * Pass to feet * Play away from the second defender

9-2

Once the game is properly constructed, you'll see the players dealing with the problem. Pick and choose the moments you want to make any corrections or suggestions, but be careful not to over coach. Correcting every mistake easily becomes micromanaging. The kids are learning, and that takes time, so give them a chance to get the hang of what they are trying to do. Also, be on the lookout for any innovative ideas that they might come up with on their own. That can provide you with an opportunity to acknowledge their input into the game.

If the players are having technical problems you can assign some specific "homework" to do outside of training. If players don't do any homework, you have a problem that is outside of your control. Either they lack the motivation or their environment doesn't support the effort. You can continue to work with them, but keep your expectations in line with the reality of their situation.

You'll need to be flexible in all of this. Some players may not show up and you won't' be able to do what you had planned. Likewise, if the "other team" doesn't cooperate you'll need to address that by coaching them. In any case you'll be approaching the session with a written plan, and that is always better than trying to wing it.

As a footnote, you can keep a copy of your roster on the back and check off the players who were absent. This will give you objective information concerning attendance that you might need later in the season when discussing a player's evaluation with a parent. You can also make some notes about what worked, what didn't and any new ideas that might come to mind right on the form.

Luckily most of the problems facing youth soccer players are general in nature. The games described in Chapter 11 will cover many of the ones that you'll come across. By simply modifying one or two of them you can find a good mix of prescriptions for your specific soccer complaint.

Adjusting the Treatment — Change the Resistance

So now you've diagnosed the problem and come up with the perfect prescription to cure the soccer disease. All that's left is to administer the treatment and watch the problem go away right? If it was only that easy.

Even with brilliantly constructed games, it takes time for a lesson to take hold. Little happens overnight, and there is no magic pill that brings instant results. You'll need patience in order to see the benefits.

Each game offers its own challenge, and for players to understand and internalize the lesson they'll have to work on the problem repeatedly. Inevitably, this requires dressing up the problem a little differently and letting the children deal with it in another form. Keep in mind that one child will 'get' a game while another one won't. This will require you to come up with variations of the lesson in order to reach the majority of your players.

As the players master the form it becomes easier, which is what you want. But when it becomes too easy, make it harder so they can continue learning. And the reverse holds true. If the game is too hard, and the children aren't learning, make it easier so the lesson can progress. You accomplish all this by playing with the elements, adjusting the size of the field, numbers in the teams, the goals, the ball and the rules. By carefully manipulating these you can set the game to the appropriate level or change the focus entirely.

Stages of Learning

Now that you have a formula for reading the game and the steps for creating your own small-sided games, the next topic we'll cover is how to introduce a new game, recognizing the different stages and what to coach in each one.

Keep in mind that not everybody will get through these stages at the same time. Some children are quick learners and only need to be shown something once; others never seem to get the hang of an idea. Since you're likely to have both types in the team, the time it takes to get through any stage is never as quick or smooth as you think it should be. Just remember that a team can only travel as fast as the slowest player.

Stage One – Orientation

Children want to get to the game as quickly as possible. After all, that's why they came. When you introduce or start a game, get it going as quickly as you can. All the players really need to know are the teams, the field, how to score and any special rules that might apply. If the games are small enough, i.e. 2v2, and you have enough players for several games; use two teams for a quick demonstration. If they make a mistake, and most likely they will, a single correction can provide a clear picture of a common problem to everyone. Most games should take less than a minute to get going.

During this orientation stage the players will get used to each other, the field and the game; essentially, they're using the game as a warm-up. Use this period to evaluate the game, not the players, because first you must make sure that the game is right. Are the field, goals and team's the right size? Do you need to add or change any rules? Swap any players? It's your chance to tweak any of the elements that aren't helping the learning process.

Stage Two - Look for the Biggest Problem

Once the players are comfortable with the game, and this might take a practice or two, you can start the process of reading the game, the process we looked at earlier. Ask yourself, "If I could change one thing to make the game better, what would it be?" Since you've already tweaked the game the biggest problem will be in one of the teams. Concentrate on that team. As you fix their problem it can create a new one in the other team. This ping-pong problem solving might go on for a while. As each team improves their game, they give their opponents a new set of problems, and therein lays a fundamental truth in soccer. That it is a game of opposing forces. It's about solving problems at the same time that you're giving them and the team that is better at giving and solving problems has a real advantage.

Your work, coaching, in this stage will be more organizational than technical. When everyone is playing with his or her own plan, the most likely case, effective teamwork is difficult if not impossible. Don't be surprised to find yourself spending most of your time getting players to understand their roles, the basic objectives of the game and on the communication between players.

Stage Three - Fine Tune the Solutions

After awhile most of the organizational problems will be solved. You'll know that happens when the teams play a pretty good-looking game, with confidence and a sense of purpose. The game flows and the players are "Playing from their positions."

In stage three the players are functioning within their TIC comfort zones. This is when you can begin to look for opportunities to raise the stakes, to challenge them with new ideas or to increase the speed of play. You're fine-tuning an already well functioning machine. The problems that you'll be looking for are the minor details that separate the top players from the good ones and will require close and critical analysis.

Stage Four - They Carry the Lessons to Different Games

It's been said that learning is a permanent change in behavior. When the players are able to carry the lessons that they have learned in one game to another the knowledge has been internalized; it's become a learned habit. If the behavior doesn't transfer outside of the original game, or only occasionally appears, real learning hasn't taken place. The purpose of small-sided games is to present simplified soccer problems for the kids to solve. If they can't take their solutions with them then it's back to the drawing board and another diagnosis.

Movement between these stages won't proceed on a straight line. It's normal for children to slip back and forth between them and this will require patience on your part.

Having the right prescription and treatment is all well and good, but if you don't have some way to evaluate the patient then you'll never know if they're getting better or not. The following will provide you with some guidelines with which you can quickly, easily and accurately evaluate your players and team.

Evaluations

Evaluations can generally be divided into two types, objective and subjective. An objective evaluation requires some form of measurement. For teams, this is usually on the scoreboard, the won/loss record or goals for, goals against. For individuals it could be expressed as a number of juggles, minutes played, how many goals/saves they've made or how fast they can dribble through a set of cones. In an objective evaluation benchmarks are quantifiable and measurable.

On the other hand, subjective evaluations don't offer this type of clarity and can be difficult to "prove." They can become a matter of "what you like," open to cultural bias and difficult to support outside of opinion. This type of evaluation is useful in aesthetic fields, like art or music, where quantified measurements are difficult. Subjective evaluations are often based on the opinions of "Experts."

Evaluating small-sided games poses a problem of which type to use. While there are a number of things that can be measured — e.g., the score, the number of passes, tackles, successful 1v1's and so on — the games have a life of their own. What you want to observe and count might not occur, or matter to the outcome of the match. This makes an objective evaluation difficult and even worse, possibly irrelevant. On the other hand, a subjective evaluation will need some standard in place for comparison. This standard must be meaningful and relevant to the many different forms of small-sided games. It will also need to be easy enough to use that even a "Layman" won't have too much trouble with.

But before you start evaluating players, it's helpful to note what you can and cannot effectively influence. Trying to evaluate things that are beyond your control or resources is setting yourself up for unproductive battles.

Pick your projects carefully, and keep in mind that your number one resource, time, must be used in the most well thought-out manner. Working on problems that require more time than you have and can return only short-term benefits will cause you, and the players, a lot of unnecessary frustration.

Limiting Factors in Player Development

The three areas that determine how far an individual can go are:

- **Talent.** That's what the kids show up with, the package they inherited. For example, physical speed and quickness is more a matter of genetics than it is a matter of training. Running through ladders and speed training will not turn a Clydesdale into a thoroughbred.

- **Motivation.** There are two types of motivation, internal and external. Internal motivation is a self-generating force; it's what helps us to choose our hobbies and passions. External motivation can work well in the short run but depends on reinforcement, either positive or negative. Players with strong internal motivation are self-starters and always have that impetus to spur them on. Players who are externally motivated can easily come to rely on the outside source for inspiration. When the source is absent, it's questionable how much effort they'll invest in the game.

  In the beginning children are strongly influenced by external motivating forces. The desire to please an adult, particularly their parents, is one example. Also, just the simple pleasure of playing with their friends can serve as a reason to sign up for the season. The game itself is an afterthought. However, as long as children are dependent on these outside rewards their development will be limited.

- **Environment.** This is the one area that you have the most direct influence on. The atmosphere that you create at practices and games can go along way in helping children to maximize their individual talents. Just keep in mind that your influence is only a small part of their lives — they have bigger and more important things to deal with, some of which may conflict with what you're trying to achieve. Sometimes talented players are talented children in other ways. Your efforts to produce a World Cup hero maybe at odds with their parents' efforts to produce a Nobel Prize winner.

There is one absolute for the environment, make sure that the children are enjoying themselves. This does not mean that you have to dumb the game down or simply entertain them. It just means that in the end, the game will have to be enjoyable in and of itself. This gets back to motivation. At some point children will decide how much they want to play soccer, simply for the pleasure of playing. When the game is fun for it's own sake it reinforces their commitment to it.

Keep practices and games centered on building a positive relationship between the child and the sport. Chances are you're not creating a World Cup star, but you might be creating a lifelong fan and an adult who will stay involved in the game long past their playing days.

Speed of Play Provides the Context for Evaluations

Anyone who has played in competitive sports long enough knows the feeling when they are playing at a level that is over their head. The game is simply too fast, physically and mentally. Indeed, the inability to adapt to the increased demands made by the faster game is the single biggest factor in keeping players from advancing to, or staying at, a higher level. Speed of play is the standard by which individuals, teams and levels can be judged and differentiated. It can serve as the criteria for evaluating individuals and teams, not just in small-sided games but also in real 11v11 soccer as well. Here's why:

- **It can be observed in individuals and teams.** When you're watching a game, you can compare a player or the team's speed of play against themselves at an earlier point in time, or, against another player or team. You can make a direct comparison and this allows for measurement.

- **Speed of play applies to all forms.** Speed of play is part of every small-sided game, from soccer tennis to 8v8 and even 11v11.

- **Speed of play applies to all of the moments.** In possession, losing possession, opponents in possession and regaining possession — speed of play does not stop with one or begin with another. Rather, it's a key factor, a thread that runs through all four.

Speed of play is relative to level. For young children their optimal speed of play is to "get the ball and do it yourself." The most dominant child simply overpowers opponents and teammates. As children get older, two or three players will form a clique and solve all of the problems themselves. For them it seems better to ignore lesser players, they just get in the way and slow them down. Finally, players at the higher levels accept that everyone will have to contribute in some fashion to meet the objectives of the team. At these levels, a major problem for the coach is to get everyone playing at the same tempo.

In the orientation phase, speed of play will be erratic. As the children get used to the game the speed of play begins to level out. It can improve, stop and even go backwards. Your job is to watch the game and determine what factors to influence to help the players gain control over the tempo of the match. When players have mastered a game at a certain level, and the resistance is increased, their speed of play will slow again while they make their adjustments.

One aim of training is to help the players be able to play at a faster speed, against greater resistance and for longer periods. But playing fast without control isn't acceptable. It can become a version of kick-and-run, high-pressure soccer - exciting in its enthusiasm, but ugly and chaotic in its result. Speed, like any technique or tactic, is a tool that can be misused.

Ultimately, the team that can control the speed of play will dictate how the game will go. Sometimes teams will aim to slow the game down. They want to force the opponent to play at a slower tempo than they want to, and then increase the pace when the time is right. This happens a lot when a team uses the counterattacking style or is protecting a lead.

Evaluating Player Types - Contribution to the Game

There is the belief that every player should be a master of every position and every skill. Everyone should be able to score goals, tackle wily wingers, play in the goal in emergencies, and in short, be all things to all people. This creates an incredibly long list of requirements for a player and adds to the difficulty in an evaluation. After all, you'd be looking for different set of qualities in a central defender then you would in a center forward.

Simplify your evaluations by starting with just three categories of players: those who score goals, those who make goals and those who win the ball back. Figure out where a player belongs by watching them play. Pay attention to their natural tendencies. What role do they gravitate to? Where are they most comfortable and effective? This step will provide a context for how you view the rest of the player's qualities.

Once you have a player's basic category figured out, decide whether or not they made a positive contribution to the team's efforts in that category. Ultimately everyone has to pull his or her own weight. When you measure individuals this way, by how they fill a role in the game and not by some external criteria, i.e. number of juggles or timed runs, even the weakest player can still have a positive effect in the team's efforts. It allows the 'one trick pony' to stay in the team to do what they do best.

Assuming that the player has the proper motivation there are two situations when their contribution will not be up to par. The first is when the player is at the wrong level. For example, a child who has never played soccer comes into a team that has been together for four years. While the new player may have good physical and mental qualities they'll be years behind their teammates in the learning/experience curve. Until they can make up the gap their contribution will be substandard. They are essentially living in an orientation stage to the sport while everyone else has moved onto a higher stage.

The second situation occurs when the player is at the correct level but in the wrong role or position. This happens a lot more often then we'd like to think. How many right-footed players are sent out to the left wing? The reality in youth soccer is that most teams have at least a few players playing out of position. Not only does this affect that player, it has consequences, usually negative, for everyone in the team. It's practically unavoidable, and as a coach you'll need to take this into account during an evaluation.

It becomes a problem when the contribution isn't up to the level of the game. The consequences can run from "costing a goal" to "getting cut." When a player understands the nature of the problem, accepts responsibility for changing it, has the necessary talent and motivation they have the raw materials to raise the level of their game. If any of those factors are missing it's an uphill battle. If present they have a good chance to keep their job or even get a promotion.

Another common problem in youth soccer are players who are sacrificed for the team. Not many hands go up when you're looking for a goalkeeper or the left back. Players who are unhappy with their role face a real motivational drain, and either need to develop the qualities required to play in their preferred role or find another team in which they can. (This might mean moving down a level.)

Still another problem comes up when the level changes, either up or down. For example, the team wins promotion or gets relegated. In this situation, the player is overwhelmed because his or her skills are insufficient or they become bored because they're not challenged. Players in the former circumstance need to develop some new or improved qualities and in the latter they need to find a more competitive outlet.

So far all we have established is a simple pass/fail system for three general player types based on a subjective evaluation of their contribution to the game. Now we'll take a more detailed look at the quality of the contribution and the specific areas that you will be concerned with.

SPIT: The Players Key Qualities

After evaluating the basic contribution you can begin a more detailed analysis. This involves his or her SPIT — Speed, personality, insight and technique. You cannot isolate one from another; each area is related to, and dependent on, the others. For example, a poor decision (bad insight) has technical consequences and a slow player has limited tactical options. But when a player is weak in one area they can compensate in another; by playing to their strengths and avoiding their weaknesses they can still play a positive, although limited role in the team.

- **Speed.** Physical speed alone is a tremendous asset. It gives a player the means to cause and solve a lot of problems. It allows them to cover more ground, faster which allows them to have a greater impact on the game. Mental speed allows a player to "get the jump" on opponents. By thinking ahead they can start quicker and arrive at their destination sooner. However, speed is a quality that you can have very little affect on, it's largely a part of their talent package.

- **Personality.** How well do your players handle pressure and adversity? Can they maintain concentration under stress? Can they accept responsibility and work for the common good? The answers to these questions play a large role in how far a player can go. Being able to handle higher levels of stress brought on by increased speed of play is a vital quality for a player. These characteristics are also a part of the talent package.

- **Insight.** Reading the game, foresight, grasp, whatever you call it, is the ability to rapidly understand the situation and arrive at a decision. It is the where, when and why in the soccer-playing process. Kids with good insight simply "Get it" the first time. They have already moved onto the next problem while other kids are still warming up to the first one. Over the course of a season this will put them far ahead of everyone else. Once again this is a part of their talent package. While you can help them with what they're thinking about, improving the speed at which they process information is largely outside your control.

- **Technique.** Techniques are the tools that players use to accomplish their objectives. This is the one area that you can have the greatest influence on, and for that reason it's last on the list. All things being equal, a player with more talent, e.g. speed, personality and insight, and poorer technique is of higher value then one with less talent and better technique. Compared to speed, personality and insight problems, technical problems are a relatively easy and straightforward fix.

Diagram 9-3 shows a simple form that you can use to evaluate players. See appendix C for a blank copy.

Player Evaluation – Name:			Date:	
Contact:			Identification:	
3 = Good 2 = Average 1 = Below Average				
1. Speed of play.				
a. Mental speed.	3	2	1	
b. Physical speed.	3	2	1	
2. Technique.				
a. Do they have the skills necessary to fill the role at the required level?	3	2	1	
b. 1v1 in possession.	3	2	1	
c. 1v1 opponents in possession.	3	2	1	
3. Contribution to the game.				
a. Own team in possession.	3	2	1	
b. Opponents in possession.	3	2	1	
c. Transition, winning/losing possession.	3	2	1	
4. Personality/mentality.				
a. Alert/concentration.	3	2	1	
b. Composure.	3	2	1	
c. Courage.	3	2	1	
d. Leadership.	3	2	1	
e. Competitiveness.	3	2	1	
f. Human relations, teammates, opponents, referee, coach.	3	2	1	
5. Insight.				
a. Do they grasp things quickly?	3	2	1	
b. Can they read, anticipate situations?	3	2	1	
6. Body orientation. Dominate nature.				
a. Both feet.	3	2	1	
b. Left foot.	3	2	1	
c. In the air.	3	2	1	
d. Right foot.	3	2	1	
7. Role in the team/game.				
a. Goal scorer.				
b. Goal maker.				
c. Ball winner.				
d. Goalkeeper.				
e. Center, left, right, ahead of the ball, behind the ball.				
8. Notes:				

- Base your observations over a number of games. That way it's a cumulative evaluation and helps to level out individual highs and lows.
- Score your overall impression as 3, 2 or 1: 3 is above average, 2 is average and 1 is below average. Remember that the majority of players will be average. A player who earns a 3 is clearly in the top 5–10% of the group. Start with 2 and look for reasons, either good or bad to vary from there.
- Consider achievement first and effort second. It's what they get done, not how hard they try. Even subjective evaluations are based on results.

1. **Speed.** No question, this is the first thing that attracts the eye and gets players noticed.

- Mental speed. How quickly does the player make decisions? How quickly do they begin to act? How quickly do learn new information?

- Physical speed. How quickly does the player cover the ground? How quickly do they react to situations within 2 yards of them, such as 1v1's? Note, there's a difference between being fast and being quick.

2. **Technique.** After speed the second thing that gets players noticed.

- Look at the players overall technical qualities while they are in possession and when the opponents are in possession. What is their baseline relative to the level and their perceived role?
- When in possession are they comfortable with the ball? When not in possession do they make it difficult for the opponents to play? Do they achieve the objectives that they set out for themselves?
- How do they handle themselves on both sides of 1v1's?

3. **Contribution to the Game.** This is a close second to technique. Utilizing their talents what do they actually get done? How much influence/impact do they have on the match?

- Does the player make a sufficient contribution to the team when they have possession? When the opponents have possession? How does the player handle the change in possession?
- Be careful to distinguish between achievement and effort.

4. **Personality/mentality traits.** Leadership traits.

- Is the player alert and engaged in the game? Do they daydream or shut down at times?
- Does the player remain relaxed and composed when everyone else is frantic?
- There are different forms of courage. One player maybe good in a tackle, another is a fearless header while a third is willing to take a game-winning penalty in extra time. Note any specifics that may help in the notes.
- Does the player initiate actions or passively wait for instruction? Are they a self-starter?
- Does the player keep going or quit when things are going badly?
- Does the player work well with others, showing respect and good sportsmanship?

5. **Insight.**

- Does the player pick up and retain things quickly or need constant reminders? Do new ideas stick?
- Can the player predict events and stay a step ahead of the other players? How clear is their crystal ball?

6. **Body Orientation & Dominant Nature.**

- Consider these as differentiating factors between two players, and important factors in the evaluation of older players. A good left footed player is usually worth more then a good right footed one. A 16 year old central defender will need to be good in the air.

7. **Role on the Team and in the Game.** They're being evaluated in light of a specific job, the player type. If you don't take this into account then the other factors, e.g. techniques, lose their relevance.

- What primary role would this player fill on the team?
- Where would the player need to be to fill it? If you need a left side defender do they have a left foot?

SPIT and TIC

While the acronyms TIC and SPIT share two elements, technique and insight they apply to two different processes. SPIT are the qualities of an individuals evaluation. TIC are the qualities that you coach. Like SPIT, TIC must be viewed as a whole, think of techniqueinsightcommunication and not as separate entities. That would take you back to the P.E model of coaching.

Evaluating a Team

Evaluating a team requires a different set of standards then the ones that you'd use for individuals. Whether it's your own team or the opponents you'll need to get to the heart of the analysis as quickly as possible. Since speed and accuracy are both important you'll want to take a tested and disciplined approach. There's nothing to be gained by reinventing the wheel, or looking at irrelevant details every time you go to the field. Diagrams 9-4 and 9-5 show a guide that can help you to organize your thoughts and observations of a team during match play. See appendix's D and E for blank forms.

Diagram 9- 4, page 1:

Team-Match Evaluation Guide

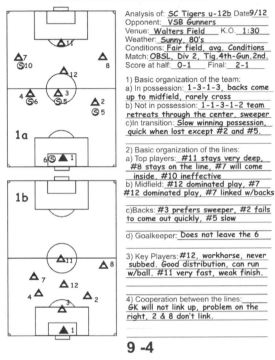

Analysis of: _SC Tigers u-12b_ Date _9/12_
Opponent: _VSB Gunners_
Venue: _Walters Field_   K.O. _1:30_
Weather: _Sunny, 80's_
Conditions: _Fair field, avg. Conditions_
Match: _OBSL, Div 2, Tig.4th-Gun.2nd._
Score at half: _0-1_   Final: _2-1_

1) Basic organization of the team:
a) In possession: _1-3-1-3, backs come_
up to midfield, rarely cross
b) Not in possession: _1-1-3-1-2 team_
retreats through the center, sweeper
c)In transition: _Slow winning possession,_
quick when lost except #2 and #5.

2) Basic organization of the lines:
a) Top players: _#11 stays very deep,_
#8 stays on the line, #7 will come
inside, #10 ineffective
b) Midfield: _#12 dominated play, #7_
#12 dominated play, #7 linked w/backs

c)Backs: _#3 prefers sweeper, #2 fails_
to come out quickly, #5 slow

d) Goalkeeper: _Does not leave the 6_

3) Key Players: _#12, workhorse, never_
subbed. Good distribution, can run
w/ball. #11 very fast, weak finish.

4) Cooperation between the lines:
GK will not link up, problem on the
right, 2 & 8 don't link.

9 -4

- The top section provides basic information and the context of the match. Was it a scrimmage, league game, Cup Final? You can be as detailed as you like.

1. Basic organization of the team, the general picture. How did they want to play when in, and not in, possession? How well did they transition between these moments?

2. A more detailed analysis of the team's organization. How were the individual lines constructed? Who had what job in each line? How well did they perform their job? Start with the top and back players, they're the easiest to note. Than look at the midfield.

3. Who are the key players, either good or bad? Why are they so important? Where do they play and what do they do?

4. How was the cooperation between the lines? How well did they support each other? Was there a flaw built into the organization? How did the respective lines match up?

Diagram 9- 5, page 2:

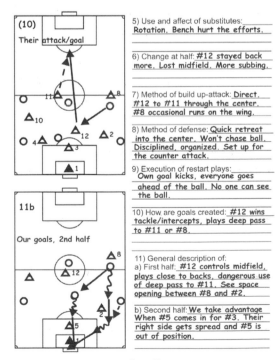

5) Use and affect of substitutes:
Rotation. Bench hurt the efforts.

6) Change at half: _#12 stayed back_
more. Lost midfield. More subbing.

7) Method of build up-attack: _Direct._
#12 to #11 through the center.
#8 occasional runs on the wing.

8) Method of defense: _Quick retreat_
into the center. Won't chase ball.
Disciplined, organized. Set up for
the counter attack.

9) Execution of restart plays:
Own goal kicks, everyone goes
ahead of the ball. No one can see
the ball.

10) How are goals created: _#12 wins_
tackle/intercepts, plays deep pass
_to #11 or #8._

11) General description of:
a) First half: _#12 controls midfield,_
plays close to backs, dangerous use
of deep pass to #11. See space
opening between #8 and #2.

b) Second half: _We take advantage_
When #5 comes in for #3. Their
right side gets spread and #5 is
out of position.

9 - 5

5. Substitutes. How/when did they come into the game? What was their effect on the match?

6. What was the change at half time? Did they adjust to situations?

7. Method of attack. How/where did they build up the attack? Who was involved? What did they like to do?

8. Method of defense. How/where did they start defending? Who was involved? How did they try to play?

9. Any restart plays that provide a problem or opportunity?

10. How were the goals created? Look for clues in these key moments.

11. General description of the halves. Anything that interests you. The flow of the game, general

characteristics of the team and so on.

When analyzing a team it helps to take a global overview first. By starting with the big picture, the structure that the team is playing from, you avoid general comments like "They passed better then us" or "They won all of the 50 -50 balls." It can also help keep you from becoming blinded by the "Star" player other minor points. These are common refrains but they don't help you very much in figuring out the root cause of any problem. Problems can be systemic, in the organization/plan or in the execution, a player or players. An analysis will need to take both types of problems into account.

Substitutions

Substitutions can present you with several problems. How do you organize your team so that you can balance the needs of fair competition, balanced playing time and the educational demands of your top talents? How can you keep track of who's been where and how long have they played? How do you maximize the educational opportunities of the competitive phase, the weekend match? These are some of the practical questions that the following will address.

Don't Wing It, Write It Down

Step one is to commit to the habit of writing down what you want to do before you get to the game. (A form will follow.) This offers you several advantages:

- **It can give you a visual reference of who is where and when.** This will save you from some of those coaches "uh-oh's" when you look out on the field and see a situation that you'd rather not see.

- **It's easier to change a plan then it is to make one up.** As the kids arrive you'll be able to mentally check off how close you can get to your plan. You'll have a starting team and the subs already set out.

- **You'll have a written record.** You'll be going into the game with a form for documentation. With a few notations you can record what you actually did. This will pay big dividends half way through the season when you're trying to remember who played what and for how long.

- **You'll be able to give your children useful information before a game.** When everybody shows up you'll be able to give everyone a clear idea about what they'll be doing and when they'll be doing it. Their role in the game shouldn't come as a surprise.

- **You avoid a lot of confusion when players are on the field and ask, "Where am I playing?"** You have it written down.

- **You are more likely to have the correct number of players on the field.**

- **You'll be much more comfortable in your timing when to put your subs in.** You'll know ahead of time when and who you want to change, not too early and not too late and in what order.

All of this requires some pre-game preparation on your part. At first it will take awhile. But after a few games it becomes routine and very easy to do. You start to repeat certain patterns that become obvious after you've been writing them down. You don't have to reinvent the wheel every week.

Plan Your Work, Work Your Plan

Now that you're committed to planning ahead let's look at some ideas for better preparation.

- **Myth: Youth players need to learn every position so it's important that they play in every position.**
  a. Well not quite. There are two important caveats to this.

    i. They don't have to play every position in every game. This invites chaos and confusion. Use each game as a way to focus on a smaller portion of the game. Try to keep the children in at least a certain area or role for each game. For example, on the right side, in the center or on the left. As an attacker or as a defender. (Goalkeepers can share a half.) This way, when you tell a child something it's relevant to what they've done and what they'll be doing. (What value is feedback about attacking play when they'll spend the rest of the game in the back line?) Use the game to focus on a topic and learn more about it.

    ii. When a child has made up their mind that they want to play somewhere why argue with them? (Unless you have to share the position.) If they want to play exclusively in the back let them. They can become an expert, enjoy their time there and change later on when they're ready. (Imagine a band teacher who switched musicians around because "you never know when a violinist might need to play the oboe.")

- **Identify your key players and your preferred system of play.** The latter is important because it plays a role in what they are learning. The former is important because you'll want to maintain a balance within the team's structure. Now we'll look at some control sheets. The first will serve as an example for 7v7 to 11v11. The second will be for dual side by side games.

Name	1st	2nd	3rd	4th
Bill	3	3	-	3
Troy	-	2	5	2
Roger	2	-	2	-
Gene	-	4	3	10
Neal	7	-	11	5
Pete	11	-	-	11
Sam	4	-	4	4
Pat R.	-	6	6	9
David	1	1	-	6
John	9	9	9	-
Tony	-	7	7	-
Allen	6	-	1	1
Felix	8	8	-	8
Alonzo	10	10	10	-
Gabriel	-	11	-	7
Pat B.	5	5	8	-

Diagram 9 - 6

Diagram 9-6 shows a team of 16 players playing 11 a side. The preferred system is a 1-4-3-3 or a 1-3-4-3. The key players are highlighted, Bill, Gene, Sam, John and Alonzo.

- **Label and number the positions on the field diagram.** This gives you a visual representation of how your team should look. **Note the key positions and roles, the number's 1, 3, 4, 9 and 10, the backbone of the team.**

- **Assign the goalkeepers,** David in the first half and Allen in the second. Now one key position is taken care of. (Recommend that you play these brave souls ¼ in the field as well as their time in the goal.)

- **Assign the key players to the key positions.** Each player gets ¾ of the game and make sure that three of them are on the field in each quarter. (Even when the game is played in halves think of quarters.) This insures that you don't have a period where you lose complete control. (You have to decide who are the key players and their best positions. This can change.)

- **Fill in the rest of the team around the key players.** You can look to combine certain players for certain situations.

- **If someone doesn't show up you know exactly when he or she was scheduled, where they were playing and who's available to replace them.** Plug in the new player/s and move on.

- **Next week you can make sure that the players who only got ½ of the game, Roger, Pete, Tony and Gabriel get ¾ playing time.** You'll have these sheets all season as a record.

- **You can easily scan the sheet to make sure that most of the players have consistent job responsibilities for the game.**

Dual-Field Games

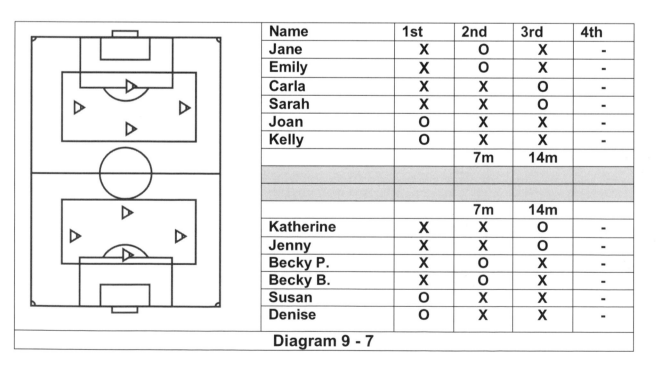

Name	1st	2nd	3rd	4th
Jane	X	O	X	-
Emily	X	O	X	-
Carla	X	X	O	-
Sarah	X	X	O	-
Joan	O	X	X	-
Kelly	O	X	X	-
		7m	14m	
		7m	14m	
Katherine	X	X	O	-
Jenny	X	X	O	-
Becky P.	X	O	X	-
Becky B.	X	O	X	-
Susan	O	X	X	-
Denise	O	X	X	-

Diagram 9 - 7

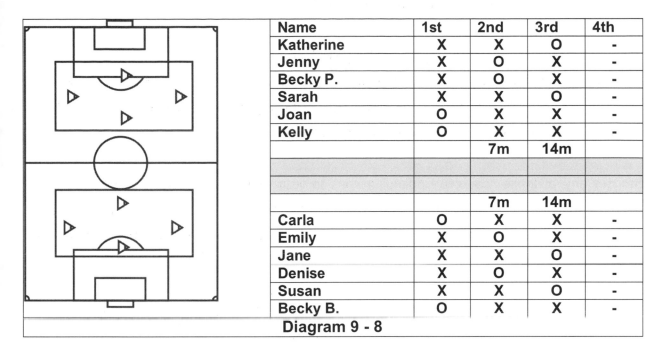

Name	1st	2nd	3rd	4th
Katherine	X	X	O	-
Jenny	X	O	X	-
Becky P.	X	O	X	-
Sarah	X	X	O	-
Joan	O	X	X	-
Kelly	O	X	X	-
		7m	14m	
		7m	14m	
Carla	O	X	X	-
Emily	X	O	X	-
Jane	X	X	O	-
Denise	X	O	X	-
Susan	X	X	O	-
Becky B.	O	X	X	-

Diagram 9 - 8

For side-by-side games, Diagrams 9-7 and 9-8, it helps if you can work out the relative strengths of the teams with the opposing coach beforehand. In this example we have a roster of twelve players playing 4v4 on two fields. X is playing and O is out. The games are two, 20-minute halves.

- **Each sheet/table represents ½ of the game.** In the first half the team hierarchy is that the top six players are on one field while the bottom six are on the other. The opponents should be organized the same way so that the teams are at relatively equal strength.

- **Because of the short nature of the halves think of them being equally divided into thirds.** Make the first change 1/3 into the game, the second at 2/3's. This system will balance out the time evenly.

- **In the second half three players have switched between the two fields.** Now the teams and the games will be different while the substitution pattern stays the same. When both coaches work in a cooperative fashion you can get the best games and the best learning environment.

Having some structure before the game starts will bring you some peace of mind. Going in you'll know that you have a plan and that you'll have the information necessary to change when situations demand it.

> **Johan Cruyff:**
> **"Of course there is space for the exceptional. But you have to see it first. That's one thing. So you have to see it, and then you have to give it room to develop. And then let a player develop so that he discovers himself."**
> **Barend and van Dorp - Ajax, Barcelona, Cruyff, 1999, Bloomsbury**

Chapter 10

Coaching Mentality

By now you should be ready to go out and start working with your kids. In a couple of weeks, they'll be creating space, pressurizing attackers into supporting defenders, hitting defense splitting passes and have a real understanding how to use all those technical skills. Or will they?

Before you can get any of these "coaching points" across to your players you'll need two things: their attention and their buy in to the message. If you don't have their attention, you can't sell them your ideas, and if they aren't buying what you're selling they'll tune you out like a bad commercial. Either way, you lose and no message gets across.

This chapter will look at some of the factors that you'll need to take into account in getting, and keeping, your kids' attention. If you don't win this battle first, you'll be pushing everything else uphill — a frustrating experience that no one enjoys.

Thoughts Precede Actions

"Coaching mentality" includes the connection between your players' thoughts and the results of their actions. It recognizes that the root cause of many problems originate in the children's minds and only later show up in the physical world. Even something as simple as keeping your knee over the ball is as much a mental process as a technical action. Your coaching has to take into account that your players' thoughts come first and their actions second; that coaching their thinking is the first step to changing their behavior.

Guideposts to Mentality

One of the challenges to this approach is that you cannot see anyone's thought process. You'll need to infer a lot about it by observing body language, listening to comments and asking questions. By being an active listener and a critical observer you can get a pretty good idea how big the gap is between what they think, say and actually do. As in any other part of life, the disconnect between these areas can be huge and bridging the gap is a good place to start coaching. You're bringing their reality closer to your own. Some of the things you'll need to take into account are:

- **How much do they care?** Some children would rather not be there. Others would rather be nowhere else. This can change within an individual over a week, during a practice or in a game and in either direction. Without a vested interest on the players' part, you won't get much accomplished. Children that really don't care won't put forth much effort — so keep your goals in line with that reality. When children have a strong self-interest and a high level of internal motivation, you can achieve quite a lot and set correspondingly high objectives. They are much easier to engage in the learning process.

- **Fear of failure.** Children with a high fear of failure will lack the composed state of mind necessary to focus on their task. It is a breeding ground for preoccupation, the number one roadblock to concentration.

Fear of failure can be bred by exceedingly strict rules or an overemphasis on results. In the former it's a response to the zero tolerance policies set by the words 'never' and 'always.' "Never pass the ball into the center of the field" or "Always throw the ball down the line" robs players of any freedom and, ironically, responsibility. They become little more than robots. The result, they are playing the game to meet rigid external guidelines set up by an external source of command and control, usually adults. Children learn to play with the perspective "What do THEY want me to do?" as opposed to "What do I want to do?"

Practically no one plays a game with the intent of losing. Children do care about the result. Yet an overemphasis on the final result raises stress and the fear of failure to counterproductive levels. When success is measured only by the scoreboard, half of the children in a game will, by definition be losers. And, at the end of the season, in a ten team league, the number grows to 90%. If this group becomes frustrated with their label of loser they might pack up and call it quits, which is precisely what a good many of them do. Clearly, this is not what we are trying to teach the kids.

An answer can be found by defining winning soccer as simply playing good soccer. When you know you have played a good game, you've won. When both teams have played well, both are winners. This also makes for the most enjoyable matches. When two teams help each other by providing fair, quality opposition everybody leaves the field a winner, regardless of the final result. It's positive feedback all the way around.

- **How quickly do they grasp things?** Children who can quickly come to grips with things will develop at a faster rate with less effort than those that have do extra work. They get to work faster, spend less time in the orientation phase and are always a step ahead of their slower counterparts. These children form the gifted/talented contingent of your team.

Once you have your players' attention, you'll need to keep it; success at this relies on their ability to concentrate. Now your aim will be to lengthen the time the players are able to stay focused on their jobs along with the amount of resistance, the number and level of distractions that they can work against.

Concentration in Youth Players

Concentration can be defined as directing one's entire attention to something in particular. In soccer this will be the specific task on hand at the moment. Whether it's marking a player or having to meet and control a pass, players must keep their attention focused on their immediate situation.

Youth players face numerous challenges to directing and maintaining their concentration. Fatigue, the weather, a mean opponent, shouting parents and a kick in the shins can all distract them from their job. Learning how to minimize or ignore this type of interference is important. As they gain experience, they're able to concentrate for longer periods and deal with more, and greater, distractions.

Small-sided games address both elements in developing concentration. The more children engage in continuous play, the longer they can play both physically and mentally. Free form games just keep going, never stopping for long and this helps to develop mental as well as physical stamina. (Compare this to players standing in line waiting for a turn to shoot at goal. Standing in lines allows concentration to wander. Children learn how to focus for a few seconds and rest for a few minutes.)

A good way to increase their mental capacity to resist distractions is to decrease the amount of time that players have to think and act, to increase the speed of play by increasing the speed of the game. Making the field smaller, having a new ball played in as soon as the ball is out of play, giving players five, then four seconds to get the ball back into play are ways to help children learn how to maintain their focus under increasing pressure. Put them in situations where they can't afford to daydream because the game will leave them behind. By decreasing the time that they have to dwell on things they'll need to rapidly determine what is and isn't important and take the appropriate action.

Concentration Breakers

There are certain key moments when you can expect players to lose their concentration. Small-sided games provide you with the opportunity to monitor each player's soccer mentality at each of these critical moments. You'll be able to anticipate when a player is likely to "go to sleep" or "freeze like a deer in the headlights" and can use your training sessions to correct the problem.

- **When they become preoccupied with something outside of the task.** Parents, school, the referee, the coach, the weather, an injury, anxiety or fear — almost anything can distract a child from the task at hand. As an adult, you know that learning how to deal with life's distractions while you're "at work" is a never-ending job in itself. Teaching children how to handle or ignore extraneous problems can be a real benefit of youth sports and one of the biggest challenges facing youth coaches. Sometimes they need a pick me up, and sometimes a calm me down.

- **When the game stops.** Whenever there's been a goal, an infraction, or the ball has gone out of play the game needs to be restarted. This restart means an end, albeit temporarily, to the game, and that's a time for a natural mental and physical let down. Concentration relaxes because the threat, or opportunity, has passed and will need to be refocused.

- **When the ball changes hands.** During the transition moments on the field, i.e. a tackle or interception, the game doesn't "stop" like it does above; there is no break in the game. However, the focus of concentration changes 180 degrees. Attackers become defenders, and defenders become attackers in a heartbeat. That transition between roles can be confusing, fatiguing and frustrating as the players have to immediately switch roles.

- **Fatigue.** Concentration is fatiguing, and fatigue breaks down concentration. It's a negative feedback loop. Playing up to, and then momentarily just beyond the physical and mental limits is a good thing. It helps the players to better understand the mind/body relationship the stress of competition creates. As Dr. Zdenek Sivek says, "When physical fatigue meets mental fatigue learning takes place."

- **When there's a release from tension.** For a defender this moment can be when their immediate opponent has just passed the ball. Up until that point the ball and the attacker have fully occupied and engaged them. Once the ball has been passed the defender sees that the threat has ended and relaxes. For the attacker it can come when they have just made a pass. The ball, and the tension that it brings is gone. The attacker relaxes and mentally steps out of the game.

Developing Concentration

You can see how concentration plays such a large role in the player's mentality. Coaching this aspect of the game is every bit as important as training their technique, insight, teamwork or fitness. In fact, if you buy into the maxim "Work smarter, not harder" it is one of the most important things to coach. After all, when players lose their focus on the job no amount of skill, talent or fitness can make up for it.

Mental training is one of the biggest elements separating small-sided games from drills and exercises. While small-sided games improve technique, insight and communication they also add the extra dimension of developing the player's mental qualities. Players are faced with the concentration breaking moments and situations repeatedly under real match conditions. They stay engaged because they have a vested interest in the final result. They experience the emotions of both winning and losing. What better way to prepare for the pressure and demands of a real match?

By being exposed to the continual flow of a game, as opposed to the stop and go of P.E. style drills, players learn that they must stay focused at all times. Not just when it's their turn. Over time they learn how to continue paying attention to the changing details of the game and not to mentally disengage when they kick the ball away. They daydream less and become more involved and this allows them to make a greater contribution to the game. Taken together this is the most practical way to mold the basics of a player's mental development at the earliest possible age.

Making Decisions

After the players are engaged and focused on their tasks, they'll need to make some decisions. If you agree that good players execute good decisions you'll appreciate that many youth players suffer either from the inability to make a decision or they take too long to make it. Attackers hesitate and get caught in a tackle while defenders can't decide whether to track a player or hold in their space.

You can help your players with this by simplifying the decision making process. In the beginning, avoid showing them every alternative that you can think of. Be careful of the endless "what ifs" that only muddy the waters and complicate the picture. In the beginning try to keep the decision-making process limited to two options.

Think of the game as a series of if/then, yes/no, good/bad, right/wrong and on/off alternatives. This way a player and his or her teammates can rapidly move through a sequence of actions with the smallest room for disagreement and error. The plan will be as simple as it can be. When something goes wrong — and it will — they have very little to discuss or think about. They can quickly reach an understanding about what went wrong and what to do differently the next time the same situation comes up.

In soccer every player is trying to ask their opponent a question, that is give them a problem, which they can't answer correctly. At the same time, they want to limit the opponent's questions to ones that they can answer. This illustrates a key point about giving and solving problems. Opponents don't ask each other if they would like to take a turn. Both are creating and solving problems simultaneously. This is a major reason why improving speed of play is so important. When a player or team can control the speed of this process, which includes slowing it down, they have a tremendous advantage. They'll play the mental game, asking the questions, at the tempo and pace of their choosing.

At the highest levels of the game players are able to sort through a wide number and variety of choices, problems and questions at unbelievable speed. But expecting the U-young's to do this is unrealistic. They need to start with the smallest number of options, two, and proceed through the stages of learning before they move on. This teaches them to recognize simple situations, a key to reading the game and helps to develop insight and communication within the team. The following will give you some pointers on how to apply this process in small-sided games.

Decision Making 101

Here are a few examples of the two options thinking that you can use with young players on an individual level.

- Receiving the ball:
  - Will you 1) control it or 2) play it first time?
  - If 1 do you 1) kill it or 2) play it into space?
  - If 2 is it 1) forward or 2) away from a defender?
- When in possession of the ball of the ball:
  - Do you 1) dribble or 2) pass?
- When you dribble:
  - Do you want to 1) protect the ball or 2) affect the defense?
  - If 1, do you 1) screen the ball or 2) move into space?

- If 2 do you want to 1) move defenders or 2) freeze them?
- Passing:
  - If you pass the ball who is in the best position, i.e. the deepest pass and are they 1) on or 2) off?
  - If 1 how will you pass the ball 1) to their feet or 2) into a space?
  - How will you deliver the ball 1) on the ground or 2) in the air?
- When your team is in possession:
  - Do you 1) go ahead of the ball or 2) stay behind it?
  - If 1 do you go 1) now or 2) hold your run?
- When the opponents have possession:
  - Do you 1) recover goal side or 2) stay ahead of the ball?
- When you're defending:
  - Can you intercept the pass? 1) Yes or 2) no.
  - If 2 can you tackle? 1) Yes or 2) no.
  - If 2 can you control the opponent? 1) Yes or 2) no.
  - If 1 which way 1) Inside or 2) outside.

The following demonstrates how you can use two options thinking with young players in small-group actions.

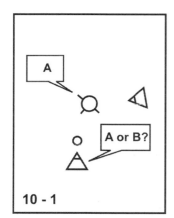

10 - 1

Diagram 10-1 shows two attackers approaching a defender. They "ask" the defender, "Do you want to A) stop the dribble or B) stop the pass?" They are trying to force the defender to choose between the two, and in this case he chooses A, to stop the dribble.

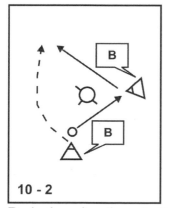

10 - 2

Diagram 10-2 shows the result. The attackers are happy to take option B and use a wall pass to get past him. The same situation and outcome is created if the defender chooses B — to stop the pass. In that case the attacker with the ball would try to beat the defender with the dribble. Either way, the attackers ask a yes/no question, read the defender's response/decision and take the alternative. The defender gets the question wrong every time and for the attacker's success is only a matter of execution.

Reducing situations to this level for the u-youngs is a good way to introduce co-operative problem solving. The either/or situation, with the correct answer based on the opponent's response is easy to read. It teaches children a simple, yet sequential method to organize their thoughts.

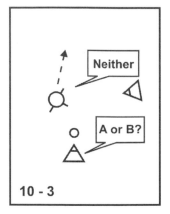

10 - 3

Diagram 10-3 shows how the defender would approach the same situation. He retreats keeping both players in view. His response to the choices is to remove one, the pass. "I'll give you the space in front of, but not behind me. I'll allow you to carry the ball and keep you in view. Now what will you do?" By taking away one of the attackers options he neutralizes their question. He avoids, at least for the moment, having to deal with the problem and leaves them with one of their own to solve.

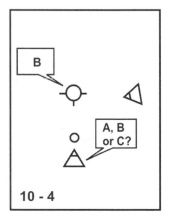

10 - 4

Diagrams 10-4 and 10-5 illustrates what can happen when children have more then two-options available to them. Diagram 10-4 shows the same situation as 10-1 but now the attackers ask the defender, "Which do you want to stop A, B or C?" This time they have a third alternative in mind and in this case the defender chooses B. Here's where the trouble starts.

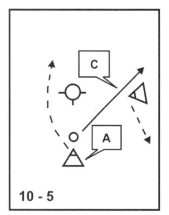

10 - 5

In Diagram 10-5 the attacker with the ball chooses A while his teammate chooses C. The defender doesn't have to solve the problem; the attackers have solved it for him. The ball has passed harmlessly through the space the second attacker has just left and the attacking action dies. "What we have here is a failure to communicate!" and the defender wins by default. This is what happens when you add the third if this – then that with kids. In the beginning, keep it simple, keep it two.

Not every situation can be reduced to this basic level, but it's surprising how many can. These are the type of questions you'll use as coaching remarks in small-sided games. Each question leads to the next. They get children to think, to consider their actions in the simplest terms and as cause and effect. And this is what you want. When they answer the questions for themselves they are taking ownership of the results. This means they begin taking responsibility for their actions and, when it's their idea, you can hold them accountable for the consequences.

The Importance of Vision

Decisions require information. Unfortunately, young (and not-so-young) players suffer from a form of information deprivation called "ballwatcheritis." This is a terrible condition that reduces the game to an area hardly larger than the ball itself. Players with this condition scarcely know what's going on. It limits their ability to make informed choices and is one of the biggest blocks to effective communication. Here are a few simple ideas to help players get a better look at the game.

Ahead of or Behind the Ball

Probably no other single thing has as much impact on vision then going ahead of the ball. Players who are ahead of the ball automatically add to the problem of how much information they can take in. On one side of them is the opponent's goal, along with the defenders. On the other is the ball. If they look at the ball they'll lose sight of the goal and the defenders. If they watch their opponents they can't see the ball that's heading their way. Players in these positions need eye's in the back of their head or learn how to see through 180 degrees or more.

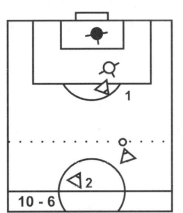

Diagram 10-6 illustrates the situation and the difference. The triangles are attacking the goal at the top of the field. Attacker 1 is ahead of the ball with a defender and the goal to her back. If she receives a pass she'll be "facing the wrong way" and have to contend a defender on her blind side. This means she'll be getting limited information and direct pressure that she can't clearly see.

Attacker 2 is behind the ball, the dotted line, and has a clear view of the ball, the opponent's goal and any goal side defenders. She is in a much better position in terms of getting useful information then number 1. (Don't confuse this with being in a better or more dangerous position.)

This doesn't mean that everyone should stay behind the ball just because they can see more of the field. But it does mean that you'll need to take this reality into account in your coaching. Players in these positions, with limited visual information, need some help in order to make a bigger contribution to the game. Luckily, there are some things that you can do to help players do just that.

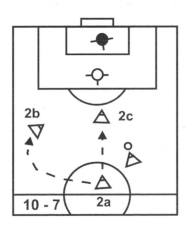

Diagram 10-7 shows two different ways for a player to come forward from behind the ball. In the one case attacker 2 has run from 2a to 2b. She has bent her run wide of the player with the ball and she ends up in a position where she is going "in from out." If she receives the ball at 2b she will have a reasonable view of the ball, the opponents and their goal. The run from 2a to 2c is a different matter. Just as soon as attacker 2 passes her teammate she loses sight of her. She'll have no idea when or even if a pass has been made.

While the run from 2a to 2c gets the attackers deeper quicker it comes with a cost. The loss of vision and useful information may mean that the longer run, 2a to 2b, is actually a better run. (There's an old truism in soccer; Attackers make bent runs, defenders make straight runs. When you consider the relationship between width in attack and the defenders recovery run it's hard to argue with.) In this particular case player 2 will have to make a split-second decision if she goes ahead of the ball. Go for the speed of 2c or keep the game in view with 2b.

Playing Ahead of the Ball

Players who excel playing up top quickly learn a few simple tricks to help them with this vision problem. Probably the most common solution is to play as a target player. This role does require certain qualities, strength and courage being two. The basic task of the target player is to win the ball and play the way they're facing, back towards their own goal.

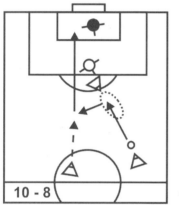

10 - 8

Diagram 10-8 shows the how a target player works. The attacker is just inside the defenders penalty area and gets between his immediate opponent and the ball. He effectively blocks the defender out. This creates some advantage space just in front of the attacker and towards the ball, the dotted oval area. The passer plays the ball into this space and the target player should be first to it.

At this point the attacker will be tightly marked with little chance to turn on the defender. However, that's not his job. Instead he needs to screen the ball, get his head up to see the space behind the ball, towards his own goal, and look for a supporting player coming from behind. Most of the defenders will be watching the area around the target player and the ball, they won't see the opponents moving into these positions but the target player will because they're moving towards him. In this example the third attacker has run in, the target player has an easy back pass, and the third attacker gets the shot. Target players can turn a real problem, facing their own goal and being closely marked into an advantage; Holding the defenders attention, and position, while making what should be a neutral or negative pass into a good opportunity.

Target players have to understand their basic task, to present a quality target to the player with the ball so that others can score. However, if the defenders figure out that the target player is not a threat in his own right, they'll begin to ignore him and watch for the other players coming in. Target players need to know when to "go on their own." This is when their teammates coming from behind the ball can help. They can see the play much better and should coach him to the correct decision, when to hold the ball for the lay off and when to turn and go on his own. (Consider this as one solution for youth soccer throw ins, which very often are aimed at the space behind the attacker)

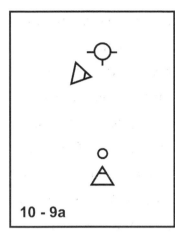

10 - 9a

Diagram 10-9a shows a simple fix for the ahead of the ball vision deprivation dilemma. Just stand sideways on and slightly to the side of the defender. From this position it only takes a quick glance to see the ball or the defender. With some minor adjustments in position the attacker can reduce the angle from 180+ degrees to something much less. (This is a useful idea when a player wants to check in or out, see Chapter 7.The attacker is in a good position to move in either direction)

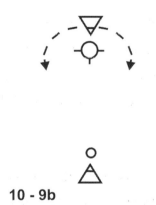

10 - 9b

The solution in Diagram 10-9b is the coolest and most high-speed. The attacker stands behind the defender, essentially switching roles. Since the two attackers can make eye contact, and the defender is in the middle the attackers have an advantage. Because the defender can't see the second attacker, he or she won't have any idea which side they'll pop up on. This really bothers defenders. The attacker with the ball can "look" the defender the wrong way and the two can play off of the defenders reaction.

If you encourage this remember that this player will often be in an off sides position. He or she will get behind the last defender and you can just hear the parents yelling "get back on sides!!" You'll need to protect the player from this and be willing to accept a few off sides calls while they learn this trick. After all, that's why it's called development!

When players ahead of the ball are labeled as "attackers" and see their job as just going to the goal they can become fixated on the direction and wait for the ball to get to them. Moving back towards their goal to meet a pass seems counterintuitive. Meanwhile, an opponent sees a different picture and can take advantage of this with an easy interception. (Parents and coaches shouting "Go! Go! Go!" exacerbate the situation.) When ahead of the ball, moving to meet the pass, being first to the ball is a real priority for attackers.

When the Plan Limits Vision - Decisions Suffer

We'll look at one common situation in youth soccer where the plan itself can cause the team more trouble then it does the opponents.

10 - 10

Diagram 10-10 should be a familiar picture. The attackers have been awarded a free kick just inside their half. The opponents have all seven players in a strong defensive block between the ball and the goal. The odds of the attacker taking the kick reaching her teammates, numbers 1 or 2 are not good. The ball has a long way to travel, the defenders can see everything and attacker's up top are outnumbered, surrounded and facing the wrong way. Yet time and time again children are encouraged to try to beat the odds. When coaches, parents and players see this as a positive attacking option they are ignoring the obvious risk to return ratio. The risk is the possible counter attack and the almost certain loss of possession. The return is in the hope that 1 or 2 will get lucky, and hope is not a plan, luck is not a skill.

In this situation attacker 3 is a better option. Not only is it a guaranteed pass but the opposing top players will likely come out to counter the new situation. Number 3 will see them coming and there's a good chance they'll leave some gaps between and inside their lines that she can exploit. (See the 2v2 off the field game in chapter 11 for an example how to train for this.) By using the ball as bait, and Number 3's better field vision the attackers can pose a much more difficult problem for the defenders.

Of course you may only have two, three or four free kicks like this in a game, in that case it's not such a big deal. But you find the same plan, organization and outcome in other moments. At throw-ins, goal kicks and when the goalkeeper has possession members of the team "Go forward, get up field, go down the line!" only to lose sight of the target or the ball. (This can be especially tough on young back players who go forward. They usually like to have everything in front of them, where they can see it. Remove half of the picture and they can be lost.)

This doesn't mean that you never go forward. We noted that the best pass is the deepest pass. It just has to be balanced with reality and a plan that makes sense. If in doubt play the simple pass. Give the ball to someone who is in a good position to do something constructive with it.

Chapter 11

Games

When a game allows you to coach an idea and its reverse, you're observing the mirror effect. For example, a passing game like 5v2 is also a good form to learn the basics of defending such as jockeying and tackling. The big goal-two small goals game, which is used to teach players how to build up out of the back, also teaches the top players how to stop that build up. Just like that, by applying the magic mirror we nearly doubled the number of games that you're getting! So if you get stuck trying to think of a game for a particular problem, try looking at it from the other side. That just might be the solution.

Just a note. The games are not one size fits all. Some maybe the answer, others offer a framework, a starting point for your own use. We saw in Chapter 2 how you play with the elements and there's no difference here. Remember the Goldielocks Rule, to adjust the size of the goals or the goals themselves and change the rules, whatever it takes for you to create the problem that you want the team to be working on and the correct level of difficulty.

The Gold Standard

The Basic Game
Dimensions: 40 yards long by 24 yards wide, goals 2–3 yards.

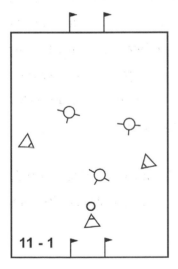

This is the game that every other game starts from or leads back to. It provides the most realistic and enjoyable way to play, and you'll use this single form more often than any four or five of the others put together. It is the gold standard for small-sided games.

The basic game, Diagram 11-1 is played on a rectangular field with a goal at each end. Because it most closely resembles real soccer, it will provide you with the most realistic picture of what your players know and what they need to work on.

This is the form that you will want to use for evaluations and tryouts. As a level playing field, it provides the most accurate picture of a player's talent. You can see how they handle problems just like they would in each third of the field, on either flank or in the center.

Playing Through the Thirds of the Field

Back in Chapter 3, we looked at how thinking of the field as being divided into thirds helps the learning process. It's also a good way to set some general guidelines concerning risk to return. For example you can tell a player, "In that area of the field your action was acceptable, but in this area we need to be more careful." Let's look at a few games that, when put together, help teach your players how to think and play through each third. By combining these lessons players can develop a basic appreciation of how to compete anywhere on the field in a real 11-a-side match.

Building Up Out of the Back

Big Goal, Two Small Goals Game
Dimensions: 24 yards long by 36 yards wide.

The combined goals and the restart from the goalkeeper create situations that players commonly find themselves in during a match. The players coming 'out' have just won the ball and must maintain possession until they can play a quality pass forward. The players going 'in' have just lost the ball and must try to stop them. If the players coming out lose the ball, they face the consequence of the opponents scoring.

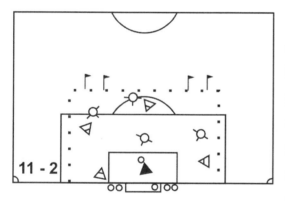

In Diagram 11-2, the game is 4 triangles plus a goalkeeper against 4 circles. The triangles attack the two small goals, they're going out, while the circles attack the big one, they're going in. Every time the ball goes out of play, the goalkeeper rolls or throws a new ball in to one of her teammates. This guarantees that the team attacking the small goals will have a lot of opportunities to practice their build up. Since they start every action with the ball they are the attacking team.

Watch how well the attackers use their man advantage, the goalkeeper, to aid in the build up. If she is only used to stop shots and restart the game, the team is not using a valuable resource and you'll want to point this out.

This game also helps player's, coaches and parents lower their anxiety level whenever the team has possession close to their own goal. In a real match, they'll face familiar problems and be better prepared with solutions. Life is a lot easier when you've been there, seen it and done it.

In the top third, top players usually play in a numbers-down situation. Playing as defenders they will have to work very hard to support one another and cover all of the open space. If they're going to be successful they'll need to quickly come up with a plan, including a division of tasks each time the goalkeeper puts a new ball into play. This will allow you plenty of opportunities to see their decisions and how well they execute them.

Small-sided games are well suited for a three-team rotation. In this case, team one is the one coming out – attacking the small goals, team two is going in – attacking the big goal, and team three retrieves the loose balls. After a three or four-minute game, the teams rotate. The retrievers become the new team coming out, the team that was coming out is now going in and the team that was going in gets a turn to be the retrievers. Change the goalkeeper as often as you like. To make it harder for the team coming out, use recessed goals or let them play line soccer. This will force them to hold the ball longer and to travel farther to score.

The 3v2 with combined goals game that we looked at in Chapter 2 is a five-player version of this game. Combining a numerical advantage with composed, deliberate play is a common coaching objective at every level.

Playing Through the Middle Third

The middle third of the field can offer a variety of opportunities and problems. It can be used as the staging area to launch attacks or as space to relieve pressure on the top players. But frequently it represents a battleground and the team that can control this space should be able to control the match.

Four-Goal Game
Dimensions: 15 yards long by 30 yards wide

Playing through the middle third of the field can require patience and astute judgment in choosing the correct moment to play the ball forward. Often teams will play in an east-west direction in hopes of creating the one opportunity to go north. The four-goal game creates this situation for the players.

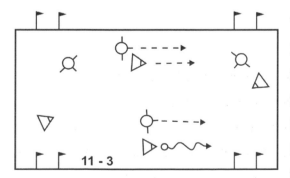

11 - 3

The game is usually played on a field that is wider than it is long, Diagram 11-3. This way teams are forced to find open space on the flanks. The diagram at left shows the attacking team using two different tools to create space: The sweeper is moving the ball to the right and taking his immediate opponent along with him. Also, the top player makes a decoy run, following his teammate and takes the opposing sweeper along with him.

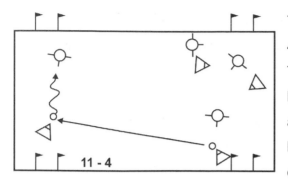

That leaves the teams with the situation you see in Diagram 11-4, where six of the eight players are in the right half of the field. The player with the ball can turn and pass across the field to the left midfielder, who can attack the lone defender. All four attackers have been involved, even the right midfielder is busy holding his opponent in check. The players' combined efforts created the space on the left that made the pass and the subsequent 1v1 possible.

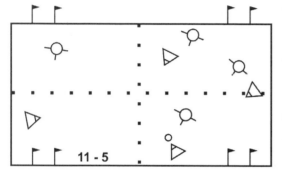

The four-goal game is one way to introduce the idea of zones.

Think of the field being divided into four equal areas, Diagram 11-5. Assign each player responsibility for two of the areas. The sweeper covers the space in front of his team's goals, while the top player covers space in front of the opponent's goals. The midfielders cover the space between the goals on their respective side of the field. The general rule is there shouldn't be more than two players from each team at any one goal. If a third player shows up, that player is out of position. This means leaving players alone to take care of their own individual responsibilities, the base line of 1v1.

The four-goal game is good for teaching players how to make the crossovers covered in Chapter 7, because it creates opportunities to switch the direction of the attack. It is also a very useful form for the u-youngs playing 1v1 and 2v2 on small, longer then wide fields, e.g. 10x14 and 12x16 respectively. Players cannot drop back to defend a single goal, they have to come out to defend, and it offers the attackers the opportunity to change the direction of the attack. They learn to find, and go to the open goal.

Line Soccer
Dimensions: 15 yards long by 30 yards wide

The tendency to have so many players in the middle of the field, combined with fewer targets up front, places a tremendous demand on midfield players. Opponents will work very hard to limit the chances to play the deep forward pass. This creates the need for players to break out of the middle third by carrying the ball. They'll need to quickly analyze the risk vs. the return, and choose the correct moment to make their move. Dribbling through cones or isolated technical moves won't give your players the confidence, skills and experience needed to dribble through a crowded midfield. Line soccer is a form that can help to develop those exact qualities.

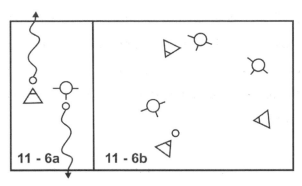

Line soccer is one the most under utilized goals/games in the coach's tool kit. In order to score a player must dribble the ball, under control, across their opponent's end line, Diagram 11-6a. As a variation you can have the players stop the ball in a shallow end zone or on the end line itself.

In Diagram 11-6b, the situation closely resembles what many teams face in the middle of the field, a congested battleground. Here, both teams can use the entire width of the field to score while they also defend the same amount of space. Because neither team can shoot, someone will have to seize the opportunity to dribble for the goal or to find a teammate that is ready to break free. (Another benefit: You don't need to chase the ball after every shot.) That makes it a very good game for players to work on their moves and fakes against real opposition. Whether you use line soccer in this form, on a long narrow field or as part of a combined goals game, it creates an objective that players face every time they take the field.

Teaching Possession – 5v2
Dimensions: 30 yards long by 15 yards wide

5v2, Diagram 11-7 Is one of the most basic games for teaching the value of ball possession, the difference between attacking and defending. It is also a good way to introduce the idea that soccer is really a numbers game and that it's meant to be played on the ground.

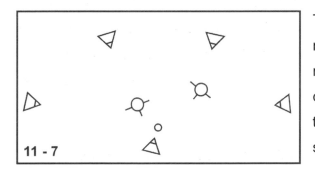

The basic goal for the five attackers is to complete a set number of passes — you decide how many. You can add any number of restrictions, e.g., number of touches, start the count over if the defenders touch the ball, keep the ball on the ground, no pass back or complete a crossover in the sequence.

The defenders in Diagram 11-7 must win the ball and dribble it off of the field. They're playing line soccer. After three goals, which can include anytime that the attackers lose the ball off of the field, the defenders switch with two of the attackers. (You can count off all of the players 1 through 7 with 1 and 2 being the first two defenders. After they get three points they switch with numbers 3 and 4 and so on. This system automatically rearranges the defensive pairs.)

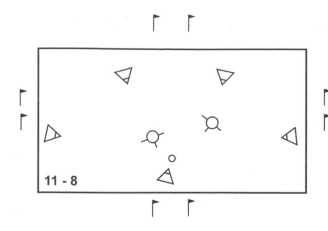

In Diagram 11-8 the defenders score by passing the ball through any one of the four small goals. Of course, the attackers can try to win the ball back before the defenders can score. The game doesn't end when they turn over the ball.

To keep the game going, the defenders don't have to put on a vest, they can simply carry it. If there are extra players they can rotate in as a defender who replaces the attacker who lost the ball. That attacker rotates out of the game until there's another turnover. This is a good example of a consequence rule.

In the beginning, restart the game with the attackers getting the first pass free or you play the ball in yourself. When the game becomes too easy for the attackers, you can decrease their number, add a defender, add a restriction on the attackers or make the field smaller.

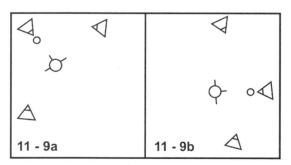

Two key points for the attackers are to stay out of the corners and not to run too much.

Diagrams 11-9a and 11-9b show the difference between a player with the ball confronted by a defender in a corner and on a line. Contrast the passing angles available to the attackers in the two diagrams: In 11-9b, the angle is much larger than in 11-9a. The difference is in the position of the player with the ball. In 11-9a the attacker, in the corner, can only play through 90 degrees while in 11-9b, on the line, he can play through a much larger area. This benefits the attackers and gives the defender more space to cover and a bigger headache.

The second point, don't run too much, focuses on the strength of the attackers numerical advantage. With over a 2 to 1 advantage, a simple adjustment in position or passing angle is usually all that's needed. When the attackers start flying around, invariably they'll run with their backs to the ball or across a teammate's passing angle. It's also harder for the player in possession to find and hit a moving target. Coach the players to play smarter, not harder and get the greatest return out of the least amount of work.

On the other side of the ball, the defenders will have to learn how to work together or they might never get out of the middle. The supporting player will need to give clear instructions to the pressurizing player, who will have to look for the bad pass or miscontrol and pounce on it. They'll have to constantly switch tasks, from the pressurizing role to the supporting role and back as the attackers move the ball around the field.

(A common mistake is for one player to be the "pressurizing player" while the other one is the "supporting player." The former runs themselves ragged, and in no time it's 5v1.)

Another good form for players to learn about holding the ball and building up the attack is the game where neutral players serve as targets, which we looked at in chapter 2. Here is a variation on that game.

Follow Your Pass and Break In
Dimensions: 32 yards long by 20 yards wide

In this game you can vary the number of players who are on the field, but each team has one player off of the field on each end.

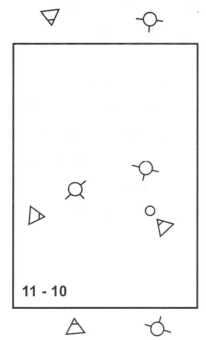

11 - 10

Diagram 11-10 shows 2v2 on the field with both teams keeping a player off of the field at each end. To score a goal, a team must get the ball from one end player to the other. Then they reverse direction to score again. The off-field players cannot interfere with one another. When an off-field player receives a pass from a player on the field, they switch places. (Or, if they play it back with their first touch, they can stay.) The player who was on the field follows her pass off of the field and the off-player comes on to replace her. When the ball goes out of play, the game can be restarted with a player's choice or you can have one of the off-field players of the team in possession play a new ball in. This game keeps a lively rotation going between the players on the field and the ones off of the field.

Breaking Out
Dimensions: 30 total yards long by 20 yards wide with end channels 10 yards deep

Using the middle third as a staging area to deliver the deep pass requires a lot of composure and good communication with the players up top. The opponents will harass the team in possession and try to make life for them very hard. The player who will deliver the pass must escape from their marker while trying to find the target 20, even 30 yards away. At the same time, the target must get free of their marker and read who will be delivering the final pass. Both players will have to decide where, when and how to deliver the ball, and it's not even clear which two players it will be — a real soccer problem for everyone involved.

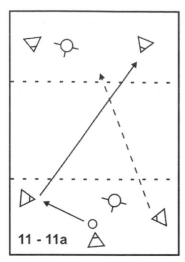

11 - 11a

In Diagram 11-11a, the attackers start with a 3v1 in one channel and a 2v1 in the other. The three attackers must hold the ball until they can deliver a long pass to one of the two attackers in the opposite channel. Once they do, one of the three attackers follows the pass from their channel to the other, making it 3v1 there. At that point the attackers hold possession, build up the attack and repeat the process back to the original channel.

The middle zone must be small enough for the attackers to pass across, but long enough to provide a challenge.

The defenders can win a point when the attackers play the ball out of bounds or when they win the ball and dribble out of the channel. After the defenders win three points, they can switch with two of the attackers. Each player must stay in the assigned channel — except the attacker who switches with the cross.

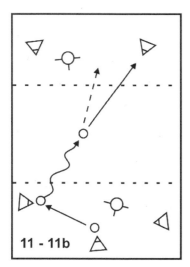

11 - 11b

A variation is to allow an attacker to dribble the ball across the center zone, Diagram 11-11b. You can restrict the number of touches that player has. For example, when dribbling out of the 3v1 channel, the attacker only has three touches in the center and cannot let the ball stop. By the third touch the ball must be passed to one of his teammates inside the other channel. If there are more touches or the player lets the ball stop, the defense gets a point.

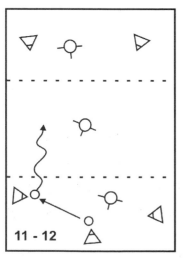

11 - 12

Another option is to add an extra defender in the center channel, Diagram 11-12. That defender can intercept the pass and tackle the attacker who tries to dribble across. This sets up a potential 1v1 in the middle. In this case the attacker who's breaking out does not have a touch restriction. The defenders can score as they would in line soccer or by making a pass to a teammate.

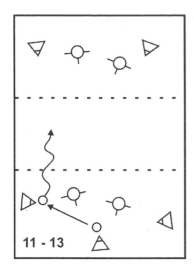

To make the game harder still start with a 3v2 and work towards a 2v2, Diagram 11-13. Now both attackers in the receiving channel are marked, and they'll have to work much harder to get free.

Allow one of the three players from the 3v2 to break out with the ball. They can play with a touch and a ball-can't-stop restriction in the middle. If the attackers are able to complete the long pass between the end channels, someone will have to follow the pass very quickly in order to get back the 3v2 advantage they have for the build up.

The Final Third - Finishing the Play

You've finally managed to get the ball into the penalty area, and you need to finish with a shot at goal. Or you've failed to stop the opponent's buildup and now you have to stop them from getting the shot. Either way, the stakes are high, concentration is focused and the pace of the game is intense.

Breaking In
Dimensions: 45 yards long by 40 yards wide, with top channel 8 yards deep.

Now the team has successfully built up their play in the middle third but they need to deliver the final pass. This next game, Diagram 11-14 will help them with that.

Set up the small channel on top of the larger one. The attackers start with the ball and a 3v2 in the small channel. They need to keep the ball and build up the game until they can find the right moment to play it to the center forward, who is marked in the larger channel. The center forward needs to lose the marker and check into the others to receive the final pass. The attacker(s) score in the real goal against a goalkeeper; the defenders score in the small goals at the back of the small channel.

Here are some variations:

- When the defenders win the ball the game is 'all in'. It's 3+gk v4. The two channels become one and there are no restrictions on where the players can go on the field.
- You can allow a free defender, the one next to the goal, to come into play when the ball leaves the small channel or when the attacking player gets her first touch in the large channel.
- You can allow one of the three attackers, and/or one of the defenders to follow the ball into the larger channel or just go to all in when the center forward touches the ball.

This is a reload game, so everyone will have to return to their starting positions after the ball goes dead.

Attackers Going In
Dimensions: 30 yards long by 36 yards wide.

This is the big goal-two small goals game but the restart point is between the two small goals, and the team attacking the big goal gets the new ball in, Diagram 11-15.

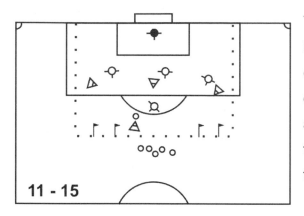

11 - 15

The attacking team can designate a player to serve the new ball in, and this player may or may not join in the attack. The coach or an extra player can also do this job. You can use offside as a rule to encourage the defenders to push up on the attackers. In that case the person serving the ball in can delay their service, even by a few seconds, to give the defenders time to press the attackers out of the penalty area.

Shooting Game
Dimensions: 30 yards long by 36 yards wide.

This has to be the most enjoyable game to play after the basic game. It's all about being the star. You either score the game-winning goal or you make the game saving tackle.

11 - 16

The game, Diagram 11-16 is played with two real goals and goalkeepers on a short, wide field. The flanks offer what space there is to build up an attack. Each goalkeeper will need to have a supply of extra balls close at hand. Whenever the ball goes out of play, the goalkeeper of the team in possession restarts the game with a new ball in.

This game develops a very fast pace. The player who receives the ball is either within range to score or can find a teammate who is. This puts both attackers and defenders under pressure immediately. Because of the pace of the game it's best to use a three-team rotation with the team that's out retrieving the loose balls. This way the teams have a ratio of two work periods to one rest period. Games should be short, around four minutes. For the u-youngs you can use recessed goals to make it easier for the goalkeepers. Finally, use this form with winners stay to see who really wants to play.

Basic Technical Skills

There has to be a baseline for technical skill in order to play a game and these games can make additional demands on that baseline. For the purpose of building these games we'll divide technique into two categories: When the ball is on the ground and when the ball is in the air.

Every game that we have looked at so far, and most of the ones that follow, involve players interacting with the ball on the ground. When the mirror effect is taken into consideration every possible technique where the ball is on the ground has already been covered. Games with dribbling involve tackling; passing games involve receiving and intercepting while shooting games can involve goalkeeping. Likewise, games where the ball is in the air offer players both attacking and defending opportunities in that situation.

You can always place additional emphasis on a particular point or a specific technique. By learning the basic skills in games children get the benefit of immediate feedback, which saves you a lot of work offering your critique on a drill. And because the games end with a result, they can see how the technique fits in the larger scheme of things. Skill is learned in the context of the game. It relates directly to the result.

Getting Open

Dimensions: 20 yards long by 10 yards wide.

It's all well and good to ask players to check in or out but it's another thing to be able to do it. This game provides players with the opportunity to learn how lose their marker and create space at the same time.

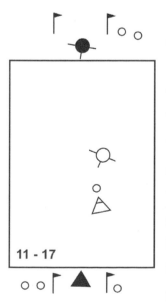

In Diagram 11-17, the game is 1+GK v 1+GK with recessed goals. The goalkeepers cannot come onto the field. Their job is simply to stop shots and put a new ball back into play. The goals are big enough to shoot at, at but small enough that the goalkeepers won't have to work too hard. Keep extra balls by each goal. When the ball goes out of play the goalkeeper in possession must roll the ball out to his teammate. This means the ball will be on the ground and should be a very accurate service. The attacker on the field will have to create space for himself; this is where he can practice checking in or out. Because this is a high intensity game, switch the players in the middle frequently. When they get too tired, the learning effectively stops. To put even more emphasis on checking in and out have the goalkeeper hold the restart for 3-5 seconds. Enough time to let the defender recover to a good position and make the attacker work to get open. It becomes a quasi-reload game.

Ball on the Ground Games

Taking into account the mirror effect, these games can be divided into two groups. Striking the ball, i.e. passing and shooting games, which include receiving the ball, and dribbling games, which includes individual defending.

Striking the Ball

Slam

Slam is the fastest way to learn how to strike a ball. It only involves a ball, a wall and an opponent or two.

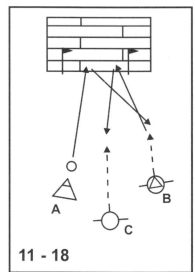

11 - 18

Diagram 11-18 shows the basic set up with three players, a wall and a goal set up on or against it. Each player has three "lives" to start, and the object is to knock out your competitors. Player A serves the ball on the ground into the goal and player B must return the rebound, on the ground before the ball stops using only one touch. Then C follows B, A follows C and so on. Players lose a life when they miss the goal, let the ball stop, they're hit by their own rebound or they use two touches. The loser of the point gets the next serve unless they have been knocked out. Then the next person in the rotation serves.

For young children you can allow the ball to stop. Then decrease the time they have to play the ball to five seconds, then three and finally no stop at all. Another variation is to allow them two touches, but this time you restrict the types of touches, i.e. they must use both feet or a different surface of the same foot with each turn. (This happens a lot in games. Players receive the ball with the left foot and play it with the right, or use the outside of the foot to set the ball up for the inside of the same foot.)

You can adjust the serve, the distance and/or the angle or add a restriction, such as using the weak foot, the outside of the foot or hit the wall in the air, a low chip.

The strategy of the game is to give your opponent a difficult ball to return. To do this, you'll have to be aware of the other person's position. If they are far back from the wall, tap the ball gently against the wall so that your opponent can't get to it before it stops. If he's close to the wall, slam it and make him chase it, or even better, slam it so that the rebound strikes him, eliminating his touch. This game provides a tremendous number of ball contacts, and interesting problems for the players to unravel. They can play with guile and finesse or slam away.

Passing Game

Dimensions: Goals 2 –3 yards wide, Field, as far as they can kick on the ground.

This is a popular game to use as a warm up in a tournament format. It's easy to organize, gets the children moving and working together while playing some light competition. It does require some real estate though.

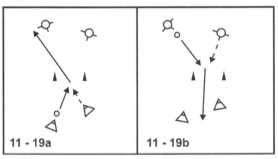

11 - 19a   11 - 19b

Set up a goal with ample space on each side. The game is 2v2 and each team must stay in their half. To start, a player serves to her teammate who plays the ball, on the ground through the goal, Diagram 11-19a. The opponents must return the ball the same way, Diagram 11-19b. The basic rules are:

- Both players in the team must touch the ball once, only once.
- It must pass through the goal on the ground into the opponents half.
- The ball cannot stop.

A team concedes a point when:

- They miss the goal. Too high is a miss.
- They let the ball stop.
- One of the players doesn't touch the ball before it's returned through the goal.
- One of them uses two touches.

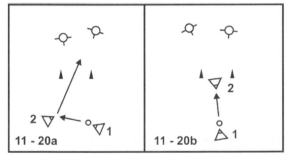

11 - 20a   11 - 20b

After the orientation phase you're likely to see some of these common problems. In Diagram 11-20a, triangle 1 has passed to triangle 2's feet. Number 2 is not very close to the goal, and this doesn't give the opponents a real problem because it's a very small angle for her to play the ball through. In Diagram 11-20b, triangle 2 is standing with her back to the goal, facing triangle 1. With only one touch, she will have a difficult time playing the pass through the goal. She either lets the ball run past her or uses her touch facing the wrong way. Once again, this won't really bother the opponents.

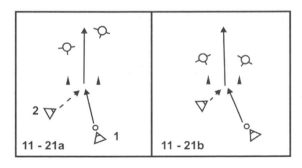

11 - 21a   11 - 21b

Contrast those situations to 11-21a. Here, triangle 1 has played her pass straight towards the goal, just hard enough that it gently rolls up to the line. In addition triangle 2 has moved back from and to the side of the goal. She has a much better view of the ball, the goal and the opponents. She'll be able to play the ball with more information and through a wider angle to attack the opponents. In Diagram 11-21b she can see both defenders close to the goal and sends the ball deep. Now they'll have to decide who'll chase the ball and who will stay.

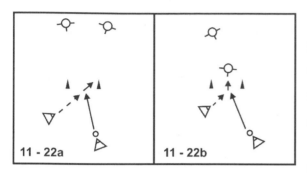

11 - 22a   11 - 22b

In Diagram 11-22a, both defenders are sitting back deep from the goal. Now she takes advantage of the rule, the ball can't stop and touches the ball just over the line. Now both defenders have to react to meet this threat before the ball stops.

Diagram 11-22b shows the result when an opponent decides to stand in the goal. By playing the ball firmly and directly at her the ball plays her instead of the other way around.

A variation is to allow each team a total of three touches, with the player who makes the first touch also making the third. This variation is a slower game, requires more running and results in longer rallies.

The passing game illustrates the TIC relationship. While good soccer involves proper technique, without insight and communication it never gets off of the ground. All three elements have to work together. It's also a good game to illustrate the connection between vision and decisions. The way you're facing, what you see, has a lot to do with what you can do and impacts your contribution to the game.

Gate Passing Game
Dimensions: Gates 2–3 yards wide, Goals 10–12 yards apart.

This game is a version of slam, but without a wall. It encourages fast, accurate passing and close ball control.

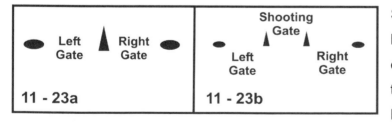

11 - 23a   11 - 23b

Set up two goals across from each other. The basic game uses a single cone with a disc on each side Diagram 11-23a. A variation is to use two cones with a disc on each side of them, Diagram 11-23b. The space between a disc and a cone is a scoring gate and between the cones is a shooting gate.

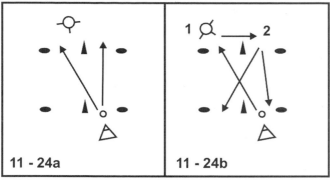

| 11 - 24a | 11 - 24b |

Diagram 11-24a&b shows the basic game. The triangle serves the ball on the ground through one of his gates and either one of the circles. The circle has one touch to set the ball up to his 'other gate', 1 to 2 in Diagram 11-24b, and then one touch to pass it back through either one of his opponent's gates. Triangle then repeats the sequence: One touch to carry the ball to his 'other gate,' one touch to pass it through and then through one of his opponent's gates. You get a point when: Your opponent misses a gate, his or yours; your opponent uses the same gate at his goal that you passed the ball through; the ball gets off the ground; the opponent lets the ball stop; uses more than two touches or knocks down either center cone. (Knocking down a cone in a small-sided game is poor etiquette, and it's illegal.)

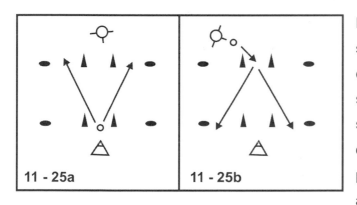

| 11 - 25a | 11 - 25b |

Diagram 11-25a&b shows the variation that uses a shooting gate made by placing two cones in the center. Both players must pass the ball through their shooting gate and through either of the opponent's scoring gates. All of the other rules stay the same. The difference between the two games is that in 11-25 the player waiting for the pass, the defender, has a larger area to cover. A fast, well-hit pass can quickly get past her. She'll need to read her opponents intentions, and her opponent will have the opportunity to practice a little deception, look right – pass left. (This is a really small, 1v1 shooting version of the four goal game.)

The idea of the game is to give your opponent the hardest possible pass to control. The easiest way to do this is by increasing the speed of the pass while not sacrificing accuracy. This forces the receiver to use better control or to move farther back to give themselves more space for their controlling touch. This in turn invites the short ball that stops before they can recover back up to it. This game can be as much a battle of wits as of technique.

Keepers Shooting Game
Dimensions: Goals 8–10 yards wide, 10–12 yards from the midline.

This game focuses on shooting quickly. As many as 60 percent of all goals are scored with a single touch, so players need to decide before they get the ball whether or not they'll take the shot. They need to adjust to awkward situations and be able to make the most out of any half chance presented to them.

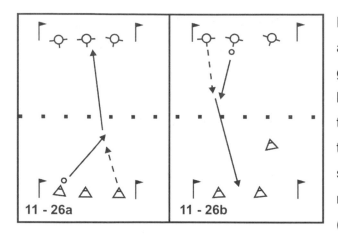

11 - 26a   11 - 26b

Diagram 11-26a, shows the basic set up, 3v3, everyone's a goalkeeper/attacker. The field is divided in half, and the goals are large — easily defended by three goalkeepers, but a little too large for two. Both teams can only play in their half. The game starts when a player rolls the ball out towards the midfield line for a teammate to follow up and shoot, Diagram 11-26a. She is allowed only one touch, must shoot from inside her half, and the ball cannot stop. (This is the same situation as the passing game above, except that the goalkeepers can role the ball.) As soon as one of the goalkeepers has the ball one of her teammates moves forward and the goalkeeper roll's the ball out for her to shoot, Diagram 11-26b. It's a counterattack. (If a ball rolls across the middle line into the opponents half the opponents can shoot it even if it has stopped.) The idea is to get your shot off before the opposing player who just shot can get back to protect the goal line. This way you're playing against two goalkeepers, not three. (You can only defend if you have at least one foot on your goal line.) It's as much about rapid response and communication, as it is about technical power and accuracy. Speed of play wins the day.

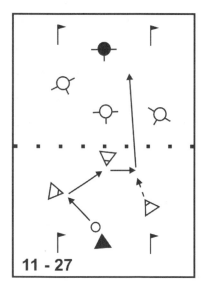

11 - 27

Diagram 11-27 shows a variation: The goals are smaller, each team has one 'real' goalkeeper, and the other players, 3v3 in this case, are free to play anywhere in their half. To start the game and after each save the goalkeeper rolls the ball out to a teammate. The players can play one-touch/ball-can't-stop until one of them shoots. Then the other team repeats the sequence. Players on the field may block shots and shoot directly at the opponent's goal; they don't have to get the ball off of their goalkeeper. If the game gets too slow add a second ball into play. If a ball stops the opponent gets to put a new ball into play. With two balls in play the game keeps the players looking around all of the time. This isn't soccer, but it keeps the players mentally alert, has attacking and defending moments and involves TIC.

Individual Grid Passing Game
Dimensions: Grids 3 yards long by 3 yards wide, 10–15 yards apart

This game is great for a warm-up. As players arrive at practice in one's and two's, you can keep adding players in a tournament format. It also provides some relief on hot days when you need a break.

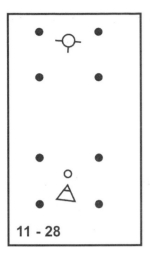

11 - 28

Set up two small grids across from each other like in Diagram 11-28. Adjust the distance between them according to the players and the game.

To start, one player tries to shoot the ball along the ground into the opponent's grid. The receiver has one touch to kill the ball inside of the grid. Then, he shoots the dead ball back into the first player's grid who gets one touch to control it. (They can move the ball for the service.) If the passer misses the grid it's a point to the receiver. If the receiver cannot keep the ball inside of the grid it's a point to the passer. If both the pass and the control are good, no points are awarded and they just play on. (Hint: The receiver should stand on the back line or even stay behind the grid. This allows the best read of the pass and the most room for control.)

Some variations:

- Pass with your weak foot.
- Use the outside of the foot.
- Chip the ball directly into the grid. It cannot touch the ground anywhere between the grids. The receiver can let the ball bounce before controlling it, but the ball must stay inside of the grid. This is the most popular variation with 8 year olds and up.
- Chip the ball directly into the grid; the first controlling touch must be in the air. The receiver must get to the ball earlier and the demands on control are much greater. The ball must still stay in the grid. You can allow juggles.

So far the game has only used a stationary ball for the pass but players can to learn how to pass a moving ball as well. A simple rule change will force the players to face just such a task.

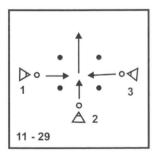

11 - 29

The player making the pass starts with the ball outside of the grid and plays the ball into it before passing, Diagram 11-29. Then, before the ball stops or leaves the grid, the player has to complete the pass into the opponent's grid. You can vary the distance and or the angle of approach so that the player will have to use a specific technique or foot. Approach1 is for the right foot, 2 for either, (outside) and 3 for the left.

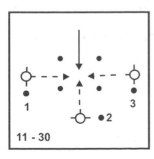

11 - 30

You can force the receiver into the same situation, Diagram 11-30. Put a marker cone at a specific point and have the receiver start their run into their grid on the kick.

Basic Games for Dribbling

By playing 1v1 and 2v2 using the basic game, line soccer, targets and recessed goals children are exposed to all sorts of dribbling problems. Any game that restarts with a player's choice confronts them with the most basic question of all, the choice between dribbling and passing.

1v1

Dimensions: Vary with numbers and goals. 14 yards long by 10 yards wide.

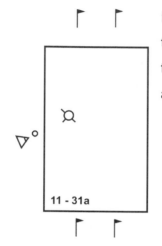

Diagram 11-31a is 1v1, player's choice with recessed goals. Every time a player has to bring the ball onto the field it's a 1v1. The attacker can see the field and the space that the defender has to leave open. They can use their approach to build up speed and defenders can practice showing attackers only one direction.

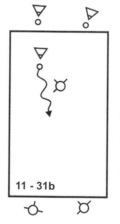

In Diagram 11-31b, we see two teams of three playing a series of 1v1's, line soccer. Each player in a team takes a turn starting with the ball, and the pair stays on the field until their turn is resolved, the ball goes out of play or there's a goal. In this example, after each triangle gets an attacking turn, circles will get the ball. You can keep score with cumulative points and after three rounds switch players around in the lines so that they have new opponents and teammates. (You can even work out a Festival scoring system to make it more competitive/interesting. See Chapter 12)

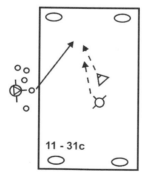

Diagram 11-31c is 1v1 with targets and a free ball played in. You can serve the ball in towards a goal so that the player who wins the ball will have the defender on their back. In this case the ball is in the triangles advantage space and the circle can press them in that area. The attacker will have to work out of this by screening the ball or using one of her turns. The players restart from the center.

Slam restart: Slam the ball down on the ground so that it bounces above the players head and lands inside the grid. This adds to the uncertainty of the situation and provides an additional problem for control. Players will have a split second to decide if they have a good chance to be first to the ball, which will determine whether they take the attacking or defending role. This restart begins with one of the moments of transition, you're either winning possession or you're losing it.

And for 1v1's, don't forget to look back at the Getting Open game.

1v2 & No Teams
Dimensions: 15 yards long by 10 yards wide, Goals 3 yards in from end. The games should be 3-4 minutes long.

This game rewards crafty players. When you get the ball you'll have to use every trick in your dribbling bag because you have no friends. You'll want to score quickly upon winning the ball or you'll face two defenders in a small space.

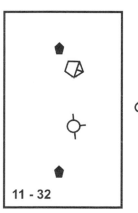

Set up a small field and place two cones with a disc on each, Diagrams 11-32 and 11-33, slightly in from the ends. The game starts with one player dribbling on to the field and two defenders anywhere they want to be. The attacker scores by knocking down one of the cone/discs.

11 - 33

Whoever has the ball is the attacker; the other two players are defenders. When the ball goes out of play whoever touched it last cannot retrieve it; the first one of the other two players to get to the ball can bring it in, they become the new attacker. When a player scores, reset the goal; the scorer gets to restart the game by bringing the ball onto the field. If the players are having too much trouble getting the ball in play, have one or both defenders stand next to a goal until the attacker brings the ball onto the field. If the defenders stand next to the goals and don't defend, add a third goal in the middle of the field.

This game makes for an interesting, three field, nine player Tournament. Each field has it's first 1v2 No Teams game. At the end of the game each field has produced a winner, a second and a third place finisher. (In case of a tie, rock, paper, scissors.) The three winners then meet on the champions field, the three second place player's meet on their field and the third place kids go to their field. Now they play the second game and repeat the process. This way, every game, a champion goes to the cellar and a last place player becomes a champion. You'll get to see who wants to stay on the Champions Field.

2v2

One very important component in dribbling is the element of surprise, and in that sense, 2v2 games have an advantage over 1v1. In 1v1 the only surprise comes from disguising which side to attack, what move to use and when. The defender knows that eventually it's coming down to that. They have the option of waiting out the attacker. But in 2v2, the attacker has the option of passing the ball to a teammate. This added element leaves the defender with the much larger problem of deciding whether to defend against a pass or a dribble. Good dribblers have more then just good moves. They know how to use teammates as decoys to push defenders into making a wrong decision. 2v2 offers this as an option and a lesson, but 1v1 doesn't.

Ball in the Air

Soccer should be played with the ball on the ground. Keeping the ball there is the fastest, most efficient way to move it around. But the ball does get off of the ground from time to time, and players need to be able to deal with it when does.

Net Games

There are a variety of net games, soccer tennis being the best known. But whether it's a tennis, badminton or volleyball net the basic object is to get the ball "over the net and onto the court." This gives the opponents the problem, getting the ball back. Besides the number of players, height of the net and area of the field or court there are other variables you can manipulate:

- **The serve.** Vary it — from hand, off of the ground, juggle, weak foot. Use your imagination. You can even customize the serve for specific players. Not everyone has to do the same thing.
- **Number and/or sequence of bounces and/or touches**. The more of either the easier the game. Unlimited touches encourage juggling but can slow the game down. You can allow two nonconsecutive bounces; there must be a touch in between them.
- **Type of return.** Restrict how the ball is played over the net. For example, the ball must be headed back over the net, played with the weak foot or be a two-touch return. Restrict a direct return, so that at least two players must touch the ball before it's played back.
- **The ball.** If a regular soccer ball proves to be too difficult use a volleyball or a Brazilian Futebol. They will be easier for the children to handle.

Don't put in too many restrictions, however. The kids should be able to get 80 percent of the serves into play. If they can't, the game will never get going. Watch for rallies: A game of serve-point, serve-point will be over too quickly. Likewise, if every point takes three minutes to play, the game's too easy and you'll need to make it harder.

Four Square
Dimensions: 8 yards long by 8 yards wide

The old playground game four square is easily modified for soccer. On either a black top or grass this game brings meaning to juggling and can even motivate the children to practice on their own.

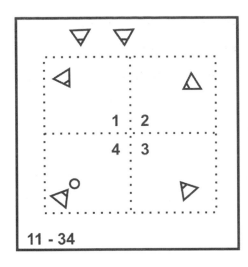

11 - 34

The field is divided into four equal grids, numbered 1 through 4, with one player in each grid, Diagram 11-34. The object of the game is to stay in the champions' grid, number 4, as long as possible. To start a round, a player serves the ball above head height from the back of their grid into another player's grid. The serve can be played from the hands or lifted from the ground and juggled. It must be played* in the air and land in any other player's grid. That player is only allowed a certain number/sequence of bounces and touches before returning the ball to someone else's grid.

*The ball must be played to a grid. For example, Player 1 plays the ball into Grid 2, where it bounces and travels into Grid 3. While the ball crossed over the line into Grid 3 the player in Grid 2 did not play it, and therefore is out.

A round ends when:

- The ball lands outside of the field. It's dead.
- The server doesn't make the specific service.
- A player allows more than the limit of bounces or touches.
- A player breaks the sequence — for example, you cannot have two consecutive bounces or you must head the ball across the line and he doesn't.
- If a ball lands on an interior line, it belongs to the player in the higher-numbered grid; e.g., a ball landing on the line between grid 3 and 4 is 4's responsibility.

At the end of a round, the player who lost the point leaves the game — moving to the end of the line and waiting to get back in, or if there's no line, moving into the lowest-numbered grid. The first player in line moves into grid one and each player already on the field moves up one grid, up to the vacated one. So, if the top player, number 4 gets knocked out everyone gets to move up one. If the bottom player, number 1 gets knocked out the only change is the bottom player. The player who knocked out the departing player gets the next serve. This way there is a reward for putting someone out. If number 1, 2 or 3 put themselves out, the champion gets to serve as a reward for being on top. If number 4 knocks themselves out it's the new number 4.

This is a good example of a consequence rule. When you lose the point, you go out and have to wait your turn, so the better you play, the more you play.

Throw, Head, Catch
Dimensions:
Game 1 — 20 yards long by 12 yards wide
Game 2 — 20 yards long by 26 yards wide, Goals — 15 yards

This game can be played in a number of variations. The ball is thrown, using a two-hand underhand toss to a teammate who must head it to another teammate who catches it. That player throws it to another player who heads it to another player who catches it, and so on. The defenders can win the ball by breaking the sequence. If the attacker has thrown the ball a defender can head it. If it's been headed, the defender can catch it. The sequence must be throw, head, catch.

If a throw misses the target and hits the ground, or a header bounces before it's caught, (or allow one bounce) give the ball to the opposing team. Adjust the rules to meet the abilities of the players and the needs of the game.

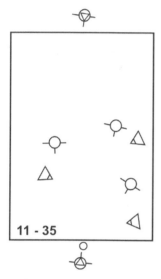

11 - 35

Diagram 11-35 shows a 5v3 version. A neutral player outside of the field on each end acts as targets. They are free to move from corner to corner. On the field is a straight 3v3, however, you can add a neutral player or two here. The game starts with one of the neutral players throwing the ball in to one of the players on the field, the neutral player decides who to throw to. That player heads it to one of her teammates who catches it and so on. The object is to get the ball across the field to the other neutral player, then the teams can play going the other way. You can include the rule that there must be at least two headers on the field before you can score. Some variations:

- You can catch your own header.
- You cannot head back to the person who threw to you: You must find a third player.
- Throw, head, head, catch: There maybe two headers between the throw and catch.
- A point for head juggling: If you receive a throw and head it twice then catch it, or, head it twice and the second header goes to a teammate, you earn a point.

You may need to start this game with more attackers than defenders, and you may want to use a volleyball. You can play a three-minute game and then switch the neutral players with the field players.

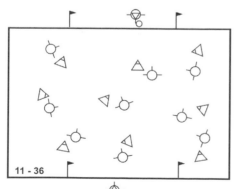

11 - 36

Game 2 Diagram 11-36 uses a field wider than it is long, many more players and neutral players as targets inside a restricted zone.

To score, a team must throw, head, catch the ball from one neutral player to the other between the markers. By having the field full of players the ball will spend less time on the ground and more time in the air. The players will need to think and act quickly in order to get the game speed up. If a player gets brain lock and holds the ball count down from 5 seconds to give them some incentive. When the ball goes out of play you can restart it at the place where it went out or from one of the neutral players.

Heading Game
Dimensions: Goals 6 yards, 10-12 yards a part.

This game, played in a tournament form, is another good way to begin practices or warm up. (Heading activities tend to get your attention.)

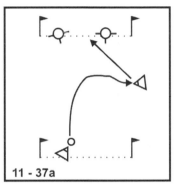

11 - 37a

It's 2v2, the players on the team without the ball are goalkeepers. They can move anywhere along the line and can take one-step forward, but they must keep at least one foot on the line. Both goalkeepers can use their hands when they're on their line.

The team in possession is on the attack, Diagram 11-37a. One attacker serves the ball, two hands underhand. Her teammate can be anywhere on the field, and will head the serve toward the opponent's goal in an attempt to score.

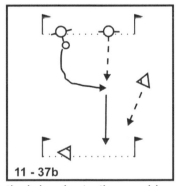

11 - 37b

When the goalkeeper saves the shot, the teams immediately switch roles: The goalkeepers become the attackers. The team that was just attacking will be left with only one player/goalkeeper on the line until the second defender returns to the goal line. If the new attackers can launch a counterattack before the second defender arrives at the goal line, the defending team has a much bigger problem. (After the orientation phase you'll find the same common problems as in the passing game: Serves that are too shallow and/or attackers playing with their backs to the goal.)

Some other variations:

- Allow head juggling that ends with a header at goal.
- Allow the server to leave the line and head for goal herself. The attacker who receives the serve will try to set the server up for a shot — similar to a set and spike in volleyball.
- Give the goalkeepers the option of heading the ball directly back at the opponent's goal; they don't have to use their hands. This can be a very vulnerable moment for the attackers and will encourage them to head the ball down, a good attacking technique. Whether or not the goalkeeper's score from the direct header, they get the ball back for their own service.
- Allow free juggling and volleys. This one's only for the brave.

Score from the Air
Dimensions: 24 yards long by 36 yards wide, Goals — 8 yards

 Watch the opening moments and expect to tweak this game. When it works you'll see flying side volleys, bicycle kicks, player's using two or three touches in the air, really spectacular stuff. And where you have aerial strikes at the goal you'll see lots of aerial defending.

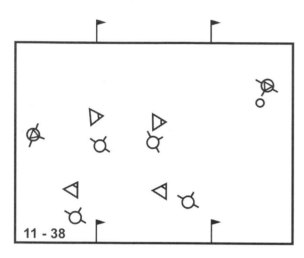

This version, Diagram 11-38 is 6v4, with two neutral players and no goalkeepers. The neutral player with the ball can flick or scoop it to any of the players of the team that he's playing with. To assist the serve you can use the rule, no tight marking the player with the ball. This should help to guarantee a higher quality of service and more shots on goal. If the game is too hard, you can allow scoring after a single bounce. You can use the neutral players as servers only, or allow them to score themselves.

Where'd It Go?
Dimensions:
Diagram 11-39a — 15 yards long by 10 yards wide
Diagram 11-39b — 20 yards long by 12 yards wide

Sometimes just finding where the ball is can be a problem. This game puts the players in the situation where they have to find and control a loose ball while facing an immediate challenge. The player who correctly reads her role the fastest will have a decided advantage.

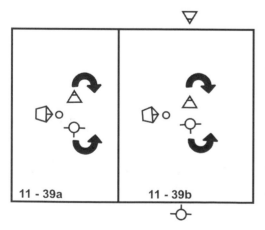

The game is structured as 1v1 line soccer with a slam ball service. In Diagram 11-39a, two opponents sit down back to back with their feet towards their own end lines. The coach or another player stands next to them, slams the ball on the ground and then gets out of the way. The game starts when the ball hits the ground. That sound is the signal for the players to get up quickly, locate, control the ball, and score. It pays to get to the ball as early as possible, which means reaching it as high as possible.

Diagram 11-39b shows a variation of 2v2 on a slightly larger field. The extra players start behind their end lines and can enter the field when the ball hits the ground or when the first player touches the ball. Now four people will have to read a very dynamic situation and decide for themselves how to play.

You can change the starting position of the players. They can start from a push up position; they can drop to the ground and then get up when the ball is slammed down and so on. The higher the bounce the more time the players have to think, the lower the bounce the less time they have. The basic idea is to start the game with a moment of uncertain possession. This requires the players to make a decision about what role they'll need to play and what they'll need to do.

Styles of Play

Children can learn a lot about the two different styles of play just by playing the basic game. But with a few modifications you can construct a game that makes an even greater impression with a much clearer picture.

Counterattacking Style: 2v2 Off the Field
Dimensions: 24 yards long by 15 yards wide

This game simulates the moment that the center half wins the ball and breaks out of midfield with the striker and two defenders just ahead. The success of the attack depends on the attackers' communication as much as their technique. And the defenders have only a few seconds to come up with a plan to stop them.

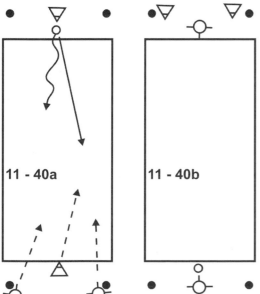

In Diagram 11-40a its 2v2 line soccer and the triangles are starting the game. (Diagram 11-40b shows everyone's position when the circles start with the ball.) The player with the ball starts behind his own end line. His teammate starts off of the field directly across from him with the defenders slightly behind and to the sides next to marker cones.

The game starts with a player's choice and begins as soon as the ball enters the field. At that moment all four players are reading and reacting to a very fluid situation.

Because it's player's choice, the attackers have to decide whether to attack the defender's with a dribble or pass. If the answer is "dribble," should the first attacker try to move the defenders to one side or isolate and attack one? If it's "pass" when should the ball be released?

Should they try to create space behind the defenders or play in front of them? Where should the second attacker go?

The defenders have just as many questions: Who goes to the ball? Who stays with the second attacker? How far up do they want to press the attackers? What if it's a pass? What if it's a dribble? These are real problems that require real answers — quickly.

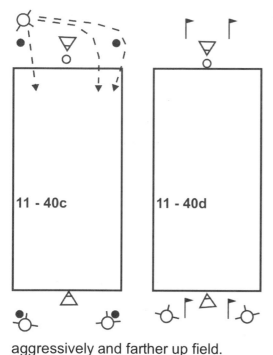

Here are some variations. In Diagram 11-40c, there is a third defender who starts behind the attacker with the ball. As soon as the ball enters the field, the game is live, and the third defender can recover to help the defense. This player would represent a recovering defender.

The diagram shows three possible routes this player could take. Each one covers a different distance, this way you can control how soon the third defender is able to influence the game.

In Diagram 11-40d, we've added recessed goals and that gives the attackers the ability to shoot the ball past the defenders to score. Now the defenders will have to play much more aggressively and farther up field.

Two Styles, One Game: Final Minutes — World Cup

This game works best using the basic game with three teams in a winner's stay, short duration format (three-four minute games). Each game starts with one of the teams already holding a one-goal lead. (For the first game use the time-honored rock-paper-scissors method to pick which team starts the game leading 1–0.) The other team must win; a tie isn't good enough to depose the champions. They need to score two goals so they'll need the ball, and with only minutes left they will have to come after the opponents. The team that starts out behind will have to use the playmaking style, applying high-pressure and force the opponents into mistakes. The team that's ahead, however, can afford to play defensively, run out the clock, conserve their energy and wait for an opportunity to counterattack. Because of the situation, the score, time left and meaning, the winner stays on to play again, each team will approach the game with a different agenda and plan. (If the two-goal requirement is too great reduce it to one.)

Counterattacking Style: Counterattacking Game
Dimensions: 50 yards long by 12 yards wide

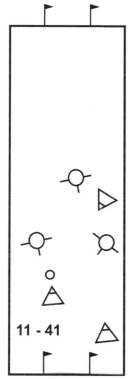

Because of the layout of the field, this game gets very intense with lots of individual battles and high pressure. The very long, narrow field, Diagram 11-41, means neither team will find any space on the flanks. Everything is end to end so both teams will need to break out quickly on the transition or risk getting trapped in their back third. Look for an individual action or an accurate pass over the top to free up an attacker. Start with 2v2 or 3v3 with player's choice for the restarts, and if a team gets stuck in its own end for too long, let them bring the ball in farther up from their goal.

11 - 41

Playmaking Style: Big Goals, No Goalkeepers
Dimensions: 50 yards long by 40–46 yards wide, Goals 8–10 yards

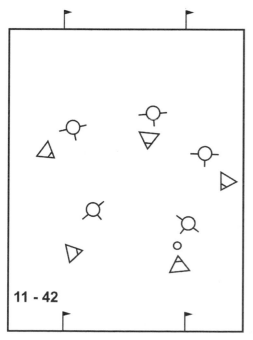

The playmaking style is based on the idea that you'll be playing far from your goal in the opponent's half. It's a high-risk way of playing. Set up a field that's large enough that you cannot score until you're at least in the middle third, Diagram 11-42. To require the playmaking defensive pressure use real or large goals without goalkeepers. The best way for a team to defend its goal is to keep the opponents as far away from it for as long as possible. This also means that when you have the ball you don't want to give it away , another characteristic of the playmaking style.

11 - 42

Teamwork & Communication

Bunch ball — the amorphous mass that moves across the field without a discernable shape or purpose — is a huge problem in youth soccer. It happens largely because the kids are playing by and for themselves. Earlier we saw how important 2v2 is in developing team play by emphasizing communication, and how 3v3 provides a basic idea of shape and structure. The following games build on those lessons and can be used with larger numbers.

Getting Everyone to Move Up
Dimensions: 40 yards long by 24 yards wide.

Divide the field in half and use the rule that every player on a team must be in the opponent's half before they can score. This makes it imperative that the team plays as a whole.

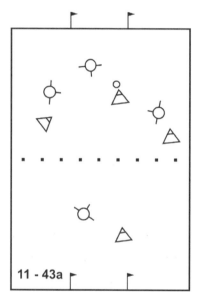

11 - 43a

Diagram 11-43a, is the layout for the basic game. In this example the center forward has a 1v1 with the central defender, but he can't score until the sweeper is across midfield. This is a good game to use when players fall asleep at the back — their teammates will provide a wake up call.

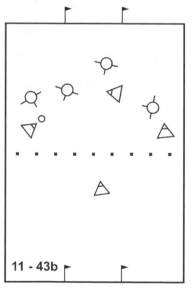

11 - 43b

It's also a good game for learning how to choose the correct moment to go forward. In Diagram 11-43b, the left half has possession and is under a lot of pressure. The sweeper must read the situation carefully. If he goes forward and his teammate loses the ball the opponents will be in a good position to score. It's a case of balancing the risks to returns, the sweepers basic and supplementary tasks and learning to play the percentages. Choosing the right moment for an action is a big part in making the right decision.

One option. Divide the field into three zones, similar to the thirds of the field. Before a team can score every player must be in the top third. They'll have more space to cover and there's greater risk to losing the ball.

2v1–1v2 with 2 Floaters
Dimensions: 40 yards long by 24 yards.

Use the same field as the previous game. Change the rules so that each team must keep two players in their half and one in the opponent's half at all times. Playing 4v4, this leaves one player on each team — no restriction as to who — free to float between the halves. It also creates at best, an equal number, or at worst a numbers-down situation for both teams in their attacking half and just the opposite in their defending half. And that is a very realistic problem. Defenders usually outnumber attackers, and this will help your players learn how to handle both sides of the numbers lesson.

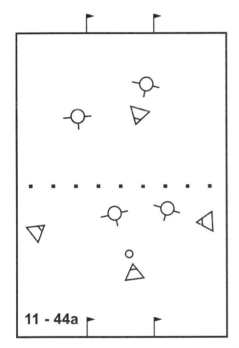

11 - 44a

How it works. In Diagram 11-44a, the attackers are bringing the ball out in a 3v2. They will need to be patient and build up the attack until they can play the deep pass into the opponent's half or until one of the players can dribble across the midfield line. Playing the deep pass too early, into the 1v2, is risky. If the floater leaves his back half too early, the attackers will be left with a 2v2 in their own half. It's all about timing.

The defenders also have to make some decisions. For example, will they play with two players up in the opponent's half, or drop back and use their extra man advantage in their own half early on? They can concede half of the field, especially if they have the lead, and force the opponents to go forward into a concentrated defense, typical of the counterattacking style.

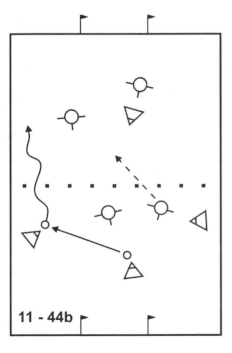

11 - 44b

Diagram 11-44b shows an example where the left half dribbles across midfield and just one of the defenders possible responses. The triangles will have to play 2v3 in the opponents half, or, play the ball back into their own half where they have a 2v1 and try to build up again.

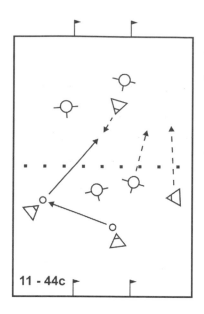

Diagram 11-44c shows a different situation. The left midfielder has passed the ball to the center forward and the right midfielder follows the pass as the floater. Once again, a defender has dropped back as well.

In 4v4 the teams play in the shape of a diamond. This game requires that the two midfielders communicate effectively because they will be the players who mostly take on the role of the floater.

Sweeper-Keeper
Dimensions: 24 yards long by 15 yards wide

This game uses the old street soccer rule "last player back is the goalkeeper" and recessed goals. Any player who's in the dead zone between the field and the recessed goals can take on the role. The team in possession may have all three players on the field, but the defenders can only have two; one will need to get back to play as the goalkeeper.

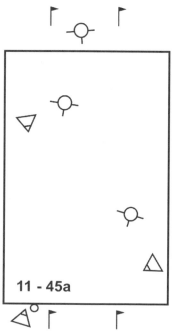

Diagram 11-45a shows the attackers coming out and in a way that gives the two defenders a big problem: The two attackers on the field are playing "one deep, one shallow, both wide." The sweeper-keeper moves to the side where the deep player is and dribbles out. The defenders have to react: If a player moves to pressure the ball she leaves her attacker free. But if neither defender responds, the sweeper-keeper can keep carrying the ball forward. It's a game of chicken where the sweeper-keeper looks for the first defender to break, leaving her player open as a free attacker. If they don't come to her the sweeper-keeper can go forward on her own. It's a win-win for the attackers.

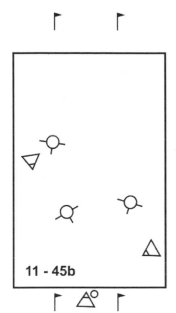

11 - 45b

To keep the defending team honest, use the rule that if the attackers can make two consecutive passes, or all three of them can touch the ball, while all three opponents are on the field they get a goal. In Diagram 11-45b the sweeper-keeper has the ball and all three opponents are still on the field. If the attackers can make two passes, or all three touch the ball, before one of the defenders can get back behind their end line, or at least off of the field, they score a goal. This rule comes in handy after a tackle or an interception. Players will have an option of how to score and quick thinking can get, or prevent, a goal.

Learning the Laws

A common concern for youth coaches is teaching some of the important laws of the game, rules the children will face in a real match. With only a few practices before the season starts, and a good chance that you'll have at least some children who are brand new to soccer, deciding on how much time to devote to these issues poses a problem. The following games look at how to incorporate some of these rules into a practice and still keep the emphasis on building the basic skills in the game.

Throw-ins
Dimensions: 24 yards long by 15 yards wide.

Throw-ins are a difficult skill to learn. Watching some of the u-youngs go into body lock, or just mindlessly throw the ball "down the line" can be painful. The game comes to a halt and the time that is lost for learning soccer cannot be recovered.

Usually players just throw a ball back and forth with a partner, but that's unrealistic. It's the P.E. answer to the problem of learning. After the first five throws they really don't learn anything more. There is no feedback mechanism outside of the coaching critique. (If the only thing that this book does is to eliminate this criminal waste of time, then it's been a worthwhile effort.)

Finally, throw-ins involve at least two players, usually more and some of those will be on the other team. Don't forget, you'll want to address the situation from both sides of the ball or at least include some level of resistance.

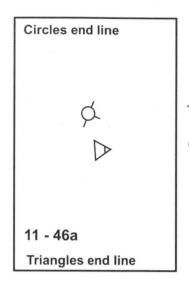

11 - 46a

Diagram 11-46a is 2v2 line soccer. The game starts with a throw-in, and the second defender starts either behind their end line or next to the thrower. The two attackers must work together to find the best space, i.e. advantage space to use. The player on the field can act as a target player, check in or check out. The game is live when the ball touches the ground or one of the players on the field. At that point the other two players can enter the field and become involved. This is a good way to introduce the basic ideas behind man-to-man marking to the defender, staying goal side, when to tackle, when to contain and so on.

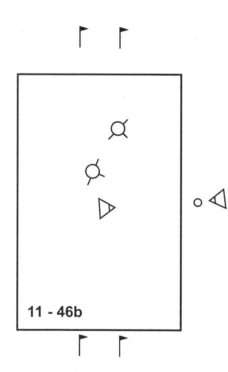

11 - 46b

Diagram 11-46b is another example of a 2v2 game starting with a throw. This time both defenders start on the field and you use recessed goals. The attacker on the field will have to work even harder to get open and protect the ball. If she doesn't the throwing team is likely to suffer from a quick counterattack and the thrower will have to keep that in mind as she follows the ball onto the field.

Offside
Dimensions: 40 yards long by 22 yards wide

The step from playing matches without the offside rule to ones that include it is an age-based decision within the club, league or association. There is little point in trying to explain the rule to children; there are enough adults that will never understand it. Instead, the best way to learn the rule is by having to deal with it in a game.

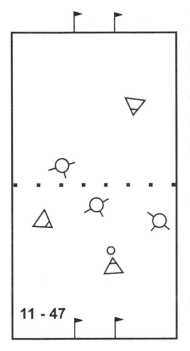

Set up the basic game with a midfield line, Diagram 11-47. Make the field a little narrower than normal to force the play from end to end. When an attacker gets behind the last defender in the opponent's half, like in the example he is offside. Don't worry too much about the opponent not having a goalkeeper, just assume they're there. This form is simple enough for a single team to play at practice and still get the important points about the law across.

- When you have the ball.
  - o You can't be offside in your own half.
  - o Stay with or behind the last defender.

- When they have the ball.
  - o Push up and make the field small.

Corners
Dimensions: 32 yards long by 36 yards wide.

Corners are a little harder to practice because you might not have enough players, space or a real goal to attack. But you can set up a small-scale version to quickly convey some general ideas from both sides of the ball.

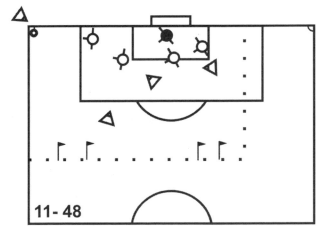

Build the field so that the goal is off center, Diagram 11-48. You don't need to have your players chasing the ball all the way across the field. Once the ball has gone past the far post the game is effectively over. Set two small goals opposite the big goal for the defenders to attack.

If the goalkeeper wins too many of the corners, try playing without one. This will require the defenders to really tighten up on their marking.

Both teams can work on their mantras. The defender's is "Their corner, our attack." The attacker's is "The ball must go dead, a goal, another corner or a goal kick. Anything else and the defenders have won." (When you think about it this way it's hard to imagine why the attackers have such an advantage when they have such a difficult job and the defenders have the numbers.)

Left Foot

A common concern for coaches is how to help the players develop their weak foot. In the case of 90 per cent of the players this means their left.

Off Set Goals
Dimensions: 36 yards long by 24 yards wide.

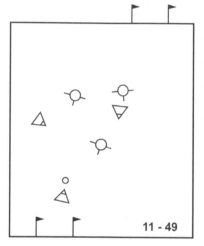

11 - 49

Diagram 11-49 shows a field laid out with the goals set towards the opposite corners. This means, that for both teams, the space they can use to build up their attacks will be on their left wing. Players in these positions will find themselves approaching the goal from the same angle as the left wing in a regular match. They'll be faced with, and have to solve, the problems that they would find on the left side of the field. (You can reverse the sides that the goals are on and have the same effect on the right side.)

When the Defenders Have a Man Advantage

Often, the emphasis in uneven numbers games favors the attackers. Neutral players and 5v2 are just two examples where the attackers have a numerical advantage. Yet in actual matches it's the defense that usually has the numbers, and far too often they fail to use it to good effect

1v2, Front and Back
Dimensions: 30 yards long by 18 yards wide.

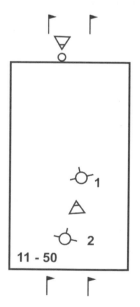

11 - 50

In Diagram 11-50 the team in possession must pass the ball in. This leaves the two defenders with only one problem, stopping the pass. They have chosen to front and back the attacker on the field. Defender 1 will concentrate on any short pass to the attackers feet and defender 2 will watch for any pass that goes behind the attacker. In addition, defender 2 will be the eyes' for number 1. As the attacker moves, 2 will pass the information on to her teammate. You see this situation quite a lot during corner kicks when the defending team leaves one lone striker up field. The attackers can front and back the lone striker.

This is also a good game for the attackers to work on their checking in and out. To have any success at all their communication will have to be top flight.

2v3, Support
Dimensions: 36 yards long by 28 yards wide.

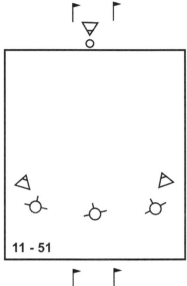

11 - 51

Diagram 11-51 shows what happens when the game goes from 2v2 to 3v3 using the same restart rule. The extra players take away the defenders ability to front and back both attackers. The free defender can choose one, and if the other defender can handle their responsibility on their own, this is a good solution. However in this example the defenders have a different plan. Since they know that the game must start with a pass the two marking defenders will play very tight, goal side, ball side to their opponents. Their task will be to be first to the ball if it's in the space in front of them. They'll look to intercept, tackle or contain their immediate opponent. The free defender can now watch for the ball that gets behind this player.

Once the pass is made the free defender will decide if he should offer close support to the pressurizing player or pick up the free attacker if he comes forward. (Since the attackers must start the game with a pass, it doesn't make sense for the free defender to move forward too early. There's no immediate threat and he can be easily bypassed.)

Futsal

Futsal is five-a-side soccer played on a hard, basketball sized court. It uses a special, smaller "Dead ball" that reduces the bouncing you would get with a regular ball. Because of this characteristic, it makes ball control easier and that helps to encourage positional play. On it's own Futsal should be a part of any year round training regimen. If not that, then an occasional trip to the black top with a Futsal ball to play a little 3v3 or 4v4 in different forms is highly recommended.

There you have it, a basic introduction to a lot of games. Every game is built with, and can be modified by, the key elements. It's not rocket science, or magic. Creating your own games, or simply modifying some of these to meet your own needs just takes a little practice.

Chapter 12

Street Soccer Moves into the 21st Century

Small-sided games trace their origins to the street soccer games of the past. They represent a return to the old-school style of learning, free form recess rather than a structured physical education class.

Street soccer has always been player-centered. They had the responsibility of organizing the games based on their needs and interests. If it wasn't a good game, i.e. fun for everyone, players would leave to find some other way to spend their time. This meant the top players had to consider the well being of the lesser ones, who were pleased to be included, or there wouldn't be a game at all.

Without adult supervision, the kids set their own standards. League tables and standings were unnecessary in street soccer — winning was important for its own sake. It allowed children to experiment and develop their own signature moves and skills. Players would come to be identified by their talents, and some would even pass into local legend. Wins had to be achieved with a certain amount of style, at least by the top players.

When it came time to pick teams, decisions were based on ability, not age. Talented 10-year-olds could easily fit into games with 12- and 13-year-olds. This allowed older players to assume leadership roles, mentoring the younger children about the ins and outs of the game, teaching them the lessons they themselves had only recently learned.

And of course, the players would have to mediate any disputes by themselves, they were their own referees. In doing so, they learned valuable lessons about compromise and negotiations. Today's children are never very far from an adult whose only too willing step in and do all of this for them. The opportunities to learn and/or practice these skills have rapidly diminished.

Street soccer was played in an endless variety of forms, with different numbers, on different surfaces, with different goals, rules and even different balls. Players learned quickly how to adapt to the changing situations and conditions. They thought pragmatically about the way the changes would affect the game and how they would handle them. Used properly, today's small-sided games provide just this type of environment. They allow children the greatest opportunity to develop all of the basic skills within the context of a match, while they also encourage children to develop their own identities in the game.

Tournaments & Festivals

In a tournament, each player is assigned to a team, and stays with that team for the duration; the teams switch opponents from game to game. This provides each team a constant flow of new external problems and it allows team identities to develop. The results reflect the group as a whole, and the players bond over the course of the competition as they learn how to utilize their talents and assign tasks for the good of the team. Each game is preparation for the next, and they refine the plan as they go.

But during festivals, every team changes with every game. Each player will face different opponents and work with different teammates each time out, which means they face new problems inside as well as outside the team. Success requires assessing — rapidly — their own teammates' and as well as the opponents talents. Players only have a few minutes to develop a plan and distribute the tasks. (The same thing happens in a match when teams make substitutions.)

While it's still in everyone's self interest to play for the win, the result doesn't carry over to the next game as a team effort. Each player feels the effects of the match individually, but team bonding lasts only as long as each individual game. With the next match, the process starts all over.

Introducing the Difference

Getting children to appreciate the difference between a Festival and a Tournament can be accomplished during warm ups at practice. Small 2v2 games, like the Heading or Passing Games from Chapter 11 can serve as the vehicle for their orientation. As players arrive at practice they play a series of short competitive matches. They can stay together as a team or switch partners with each new game. This is a useful method for getting players mentally from wherever they were coming from to the practice.

The following formats represent valuable tools for teams, clubs or Associations. They allow players the freedom to practice their leadership skills in a small-scale competitive environment that is also a lot of fun. They also free you up to observe the player's interactions in different situations and environments.

Setting up the Festival

You'll want to stay with a single form, and one the players are familiar with, throughout the festival. Begin by choosing what the game you'll use, i.e. the basic game, with recessed goals, line soccer and so on. Settle on the numbers per side — 3v3, 4v4. Once you've made these decisions and you have a rough idea how many kids you're expecting, set up enough fields to accommodate everyone.

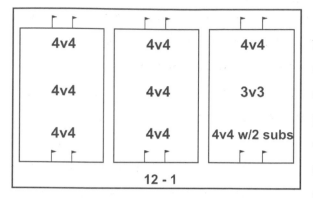

12 - 1

Diagram 12-1 shows three examples. If you have 24 players playing 4v4, you will need three fields, the top line. If there is an uneven number, designate one field to handle the difference. If you wanted to play 4v4 but you only have 22 players still set up three fields — sixteen players would play 4v4 and six would play 3v3, the middle line. Everyone will still get plenty of 4v4 action and no one will have to wait or stand around. If there are a few extra players one or two teams can carry a sub, the bottom line. To reduce confusion pick one goal on the field and the team defending it will carry the sub. Because the games are so short try to avoid any team carrying more than one sub.

It helps to have a stopwatch at every field that has substitutes on it. As soon as the players can understand how to use it they should be given the job of monitoring their own sub patterns. They can rotate every two minutes and switch on the fly.

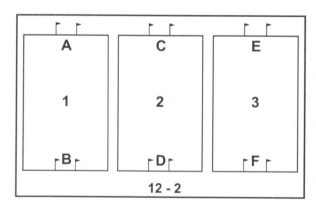

12 - 2

Number the fields and label the goals, Diagram 12-2. Leave a set of pinnies (vests) at one goal on each field. Try to keep the pinnies on one side, i.e. at goals A, C and E. Hint: Leave some contrasting colors there as well. A player who's wearing a red shirt and playing against a team wearing red pinnies will have a different color to change into. Now you can set up the teams.

4v4 Festival Schedule		Game I		Game II			Game III			Game IV			Game V			
Num.	Name	Team	Points	Team	Points	Cum. Pts.	Team	Points	Cum. Pts	Team	Points	Cum. Pts.	Team	Points	Total Points	Finish
1	Jack	A	13	C	7	20	B	12	32	D	13	45	A	1	46	4
2	Peter	B	2	A	13	15	B	12	27	C	2	29	D	12	41	6
3	James	C	6	A	13	19	D	12	31	B	12	43	B	13	56	1
4	Coby	B	2	C	7	9	C	1	10	C	2	12	C	0	12	16
5	Dave R.	A	13	B	0	13	A	1	14	A	0	14	D	12	26	10
6	Larry	D	6	D	7	13	A	1	14	A	0	14	D	12	26	10
7	Roger	C	6	B	0	6	D	12	18	B	12	30	D	12	42	5
8	Chris	C	6	A	13	19	B	12	31	C	2	33	A	1	34	8
9	Gene	B	2	D	7	9	C	1	10	B	12	22	A	1	23	13
10	Dave C.	A	13	B	0	13	C	1	14	D	13	27	A	1	28	9
11	Mike	D	6	C	7	13	D	12	25	D	13	38	B	13	51	2
12	Brian	C	6	C	7	13	B	12	25	A	0	25	C	0	25	12
13	Pat	D	6	D	7	13	A	1	14	C	2	16	C	0	16	15
14	John	A	13	A	13	26	D	12	38	A	0	38	B	13	51	2
15	Keith	D	6	B	0	6	C	1	7	D	13	20	C	0	20	14
16	Ezra	B	2	D	7	9	A	1	10	B	12	22	B	13	35	7

12-3

Diagram 12-3 shows an example using 16 players in 4v4 on two fields. Assign each player in game 1 to a goal, (under the column - Team.) Tell each player the goal they need to go to so they can put their team together. The teams at the Pinnie goals get dressed. A timekeeper starts and ends all of the games simultaneously#. At the end of each game one player from each team reports the score to a scorekeeper who records them, Diagram 12-4.

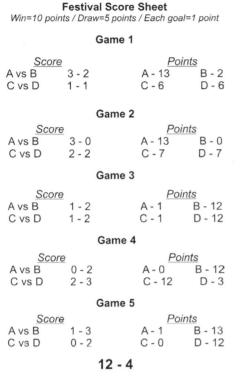

Festival Score Sheet
Win=10 points / Draw=5 points / Each goal=1 point

Game 1

Score			Points	
A vs B	3 - 2		A - 13	B - 2
C vs D	1 - 1		C - 6	D - 6

Game 2

Score			Points	
A vs B	3 - 0		A - 13	B - 0
C vs D	2 - 2		C - 7	D - 7

Game 3

Score			Points	
A vs B	1 - 2		A - 1	B - 12
C vs D	1 - 2		C - 1	D - 12

Game 4

Score			Points	
A vs B	0 - 2		A - 0	B - 12
C vs D	2 - 3		C - 12	D - 3

Game 5

Score			Points	
A vs B	1 - 3		A - 1	B - 13
C vs D	0 - 2		C - 0	D - 12

12 - 4

The results from the first game were, A beat B 3-2 while C and D tied 1-1. Now compute the points that everyone gets. When a team wins every player gets 10 points for the win and 1 for each goal. In case of a draw every player gets 5 points plus 1 for each goal and in the case of a loss every player gets 1 point for any goal that the team scored. In Game One every player on A gets 13 points, every player on B gets 2 and every player on C and D gets 6. The points are entered into the Game One point's column of the Festival Schedule, Diagram 12-3. Keep the players in the dark as to where they stand early on. You can watch the cumulative points and make up teams based on that.

By quickly doing the math during the games, you will be able to see who's not doing so well and who's doing very well. Use this knowledge to adjust and balance the teams, ensuring the bottom is not too far from the top. You can also reserve the last game for a championship, pitting the top players against each other in a winner-takes-all match.

In a perfect world you can set up teams/matches ahead of time*. If you can't, make the teams for the next game while they're busy playing, i.e. make up Game Two while they're playing Game One. After each game give everyone his or her new goal to go to/team to play on and the process repeats itself. Once the children are use to the format and understand the layout of the fields you can easily fit six or seven 10-minute games into a 90-minute session. That's a very good return on your investment of time.

The timekeeper can start the games when the first game is ready to start. The games/fields that aren't ready will lose time, which is strong motivator for all players to get to the field and get organized. If one or more of the fields are far from the others send those teams out first.

*If you're not keeping score an option is to have everyone line up and simply count them off to form teams. Then, when they line up for each subsequent game, make sure no one stands next to someone they were next to in a previous line up. This is a fast way to get the teams picked, but you don't have as much control in the match ups as with the first method. And remember: the smart players will make it work to their benefit.

When players arrive late or leave early, it's easy to work them into a game or pull a sub over from another game to fill in. In the ideal world the players would do all of this themselves. In the beginning you and some other adults will need to watch over the proceedings. However, as the players become more familiar with the process you should begin to grant them greater control.

The Basic Rules

1. **Time.** 10-minute games. Short enough to get in an adequate number of games, yet long enough to allow for drama and comebacks.
2. **Numbers.** Whatever serves your purpose.
3. **The game.** Everyone should be familiar with and play the same game. If it's a new game, the players will be confronted with the teambuilding problems while they are in the orientation phase. This will prove to be very difficult and the games will be sloppy at best.
4. **Starts and restarts.** Pinny team starts the game with the ball. Choose whatever restarts you want, just keep it simple. If in doubt use the players choice.
5. **Players, ref themselves.** If they want to argue calls and lose game time, let them. They'll quickly figure out that it's not worth it and that is an important lesson in itself. Arguing slows down the game and shows a loss of concentration.
6. **Team balance.** If you have mixed ages or levels, i.e. ten year olds playing with twelve year olds, travel with rec., put the groups on separate control sheets. Work out a ratio for balancing the teams in each game and divide the players accordingly. Example; if you have 24 player's, (Three games @ 4v4) made up of 12 travel-level players with 12 rec. players, list the two groups on separate control sheets. You can play the first game where all six teams have two travel and two rec. players each. The next game could have four teams with three travel and one rec. player playing against each other while the other two teams would have four rec. players each. This helps to keep the games and competition balanced. Inevitably you'll have a few games that are a blow out. Luckily, they are over quickly and you can work things out after that.

The Multi-Game Tournament

What makes the Multi-Tournament Format different from the Festival and ordinary tournaments is that the teams stay together and rotate through different games. They can play against the same or different opponents. As in the Festival Format, it's important that the players are already familiar with the games. This is not the best time to introduce a new game or take time to explain a complicated rule.

Setting up the Fields

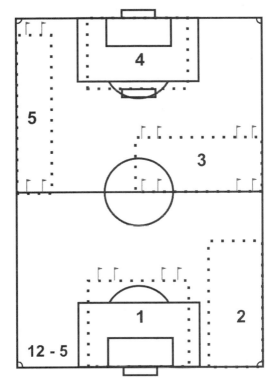

Diagram 12-5 shows an example of a Multi-Game Tournament set up using five different games:

- Field 1 is the Big Goals, Two Small Goals Game.
- Field 2 is Line Soccer.
- Field 3 is the Four Goal Game.
- Field 4 is the Shooting Game.
- Field 5 is the Counterattacking Game.

This example shows how 40 to 43 players can play on one full-sized field. This is a practical use of space and time. When two or three teams share a field for training, there's the opportunity to stage either this tournament or a festival in lieu of a regular practice or full field scrimmage. With a little planning, these tournaments offer a valuable resource for any club looking for ways to maximize its field space and add a level of consistency to its program.

Bonus: The Tournament Format can provide an incentive for teams to master a number of different forms. When players know that they'll be playing in a "Tournament" on the 1ºt and 15th of each month against other team's they'll find some additional reasons to master each game.

The Basic Rules

1. **Time.** Play 10-minute games, without changing sides — except Field 1, the Big Goal, Two Small Goals Game. This game requires both teams to play in each direction, so play two 5-minute halves and switch sides.
2. **Games 1 and 4 can have permanent goalkeepers who stay on site or each team can supply their own.**
3. **A timekeeper will start and end all of the games at the same time.**
4. **Players, referee themselves.**
5. **Restarts.** Your choice except games 1 and 4. The goalkeepers restart those.
6. **Scoring.** Teams get 5 points for a win, 3 for a tie, 0 for a loss and 1 for each goal scored. See option below#.
7. **Teams stay together.** Teams rotate to a new field for the next game. They can play the same opponent in the new game, or a different opponent. (See rotation schedule below.)
8. **Rotation.** Using the schedule below, set the teams up by color. The best system is to use two different colors of pinnies. Teams on the left of the column - A, C, E, G and I are in one color. Teams on the right - B, D, F, H, and J are in a different color. Teams keep their colors for the entire tournament.

Games						
F		**1**	**2**	**3**	**4**	**5**
I	**1**	A vs. B	I vs. D	G vs. F	E vs. H	C vs. J
e	**2**	C vs. D	A vs. F	I vs. H	G vs. J	E vs. B
l	**3**	E vs. F	C vs. H	A vs. J	I vs. B	G vs. D
d	**4**	G vs. H	E vs. J	C vs. B	A vs. D	I vs. F
s	**5**	I vs. J	G vs. B	E vs. D	C vs. F	A vs. H

Teams play their first game as shown in column 1. A vs. B on field 1; C vs. D on field 2; E vs. F on field 3; G vs. H on field 4 and I vs. J on field 5.

After each game, the teams in the left column, A, C, E, G and I move down one row, and the teams in the right column, B, D, F, H and J move up one row. The exceptions are the bottom team from the left column and the top team from the right column, which move to opposite ends of the table. Doing it this way rotates each team through every field, where, if it's an odd number of games, they'll find a new opponent. If both teams rotate in the same direction on the schedule, they'll move together to a new field and game.

#This rotation allows you two ways to conduct the competition scoring. Each team can play on its own and collect points for its individual record. Or, you can have two "super teams" that combine all of their results. In that case it's the Left teams A, C, E, G and I vs. the Right teams B, D, F, H, and J from Column 1.

And there's another tie in to street soccer. It's easy to employ older/better players as coaches — in this format 10 would be ideal . You could put one older/better player as a captain on each team; it would be the captain's responsibility to coach the younger players through each game. If you have fewer than 10 older/better players, assign them to specific fields. If necessary, the younger children could play with a substitute on those fields. If you have too many older/better players they can substitute for each other. The point will be to keep a level of parity within the games and avoid stacked teams.

Doing this within a club is one way to bring the travel and house sides closer together. The u-12 travel players can be the coaches in a 5 game, u-10 house Tournament. Both travel and house coaches who think that this is a waste of their training time will need to be educated about the benefits that all of the players will derive. The travel coaches can talk about evaluating, planning, leadership and responsibility with their players. The house coaches can use the travel players as examples of what the house players can look forward too. At the least, it can bring both groups together for a common, mutually beneficial experience.

Coaching

Please refrain from offering too much advice, i.e. coaching. It's up to the children to organize themselves, deal with the soccer problems they encounter and to take responsibility for their play. You can always ask them later why they did something, pushing them to explain their thinking and helping you to understand how they see the game. (Sometimes children don't always play the strongest team. They may choose to play in a way that is not in the best interest of winning a particular match. If they have a good reason — for example, they may tell you, "Jane hasn't scored so we're letting her play up top" — respect it, even if you know Jane couldn't hit the broad side of a barn.) They may have something bigger in mind then the final score.

The major advantage of these forms can be seen after the children have played it a few times and know what to expect. They'll start slow, in the orientation phase, but as they get used to it and come to understand you're not going to second-guess them, they will assume greater responsibility for their own teams and their performance. Properly managed it is as close to street soccer as you can get.

A coach had to make a choice between two players. The first was technically the best player he had ever seen. But he was never in the right place at the right time. The second was technically only average, but he was always in the right place at the right time. He chose the second. When asked why, he answered, "The one with technique can do nothing with it. The one who is where he should be can do something. Something always trumps nothing."

Chapter 13

Odds and Ends

This last chapter represents what I experience as I'm driving home from many of the coaching courses that I have given. It's the 20/20 hindsight of "Oh, I should have said…" or "I should have covered…" or "…would have been a much better explanation." Even after spending 16 hours together you always feel like you left something out. So, in an effort to be as complete as possible here is a recap of some of the earlier ideas along with a few new ones as well.

Coaching tips

- Arrive at practice with a written lesson plan in hand. It should include the basic organization of each activity. The progression of the activities and what are the key coaching points that you'll be looking for.

- Start practices with REALLY small games. Your players rarely arrive for practice at the same time. Chances are it will be individually or in small car pool groups. Have small games, i.e. 2v2 mini tournaments, four square, 1v2 w/no teams or slam set up so that the first ones there can start playing while the others arrive. Then feed the new arrivals in as substitutes until there are enough to start another game. It serves as a reward for the early birds and begins the warm up by getting them moving and out of the school mind set and into the soccer one.

- A few suggestions for laying out the fields.

  - Laying down the first line of discs keep your eyes on a stationary object in the distance. Have a set distance in mind how far you want to go and find a multiple of that distance, i.e. 24 yards can be divided by 2, 3, 4, 6, 8 or 12-yard increments. The number you choose will determine the distance between the discs. Using too many discs can be as bad as too using too few.

  - Pace off and count by your set number. Set a disc down every time you get to your number using the same hand. If you switch hands the line will zig-zag behind you.

  - When you reach the end of the line look back and ask yourself, "will that distance work with this group?" If not make an adjustment. If you've been counting in 6-yard intervals and you want to lengthen it by 4 yards go ahead and make the last segment 4 yards. Likewise you can shorten up the last segment.

  - Look across the field, find your stationary object and begin pacing the second line. Since there is likely to be a difference between the width and length of a field you can use different distances between the discs i.e. 8 yards on the long side and 6 on the short. Repeat for the third line using the same measure as the first.

  - The distance of the fourth line should be equal to the second. If not, you have a problem with the angle in one of the lines.

- Set your goals up. When you have evenly spaced discs, finding the center of the line requires either finding either the center disc or the space between the two middle discs. This makes finding the midfield line easy as well.

- Taking the time to pace off the field systematically pays off in the long run. It provides consistency, allows for quick computations for adjustments and helps you remember what sizes generally work best.

- Use different colored discs to mean something. Using a different colored disc as the end line in line soccer gives kids a visual cue. Alternating the colors of fields in your opening really small games facilitates organization.

- Fix the game before you try fixing the players. If the games not working fix it first. (Remember the Goldielocks rule.) If you have to reduce or increase the numbers go ahead. If the field conditions don't allow the team to play the way you want you'll need to make an allowance or abandon the idea altogether.

- Don't stop the game to change the field size. Make your adjustments while they're playing. Simply walk along the sides or ends and adjust the discs, or, set a new line down and then go back and pick up the original line. There's usually no need to stop the game.

- When you have the players gather around you for a talk make sure that there is nothing interesting happening behind you. If the kids can see something interesting, like another game, you'll have to repeat yourself. If there's a hill, they can sit at the bottom of it and look into it while you stand slightly uphill. Look for a neutral or passive background to keep behind you and make sure that they are not looking into the sun.

- With the u-youngs, get down to their level when you talk with them. This will help make them more comfortable and help you to appreciate the world from their perspective.

- The freeze technique. As you're watching the team play you can freeze the game when you observe something going wrong. Just yell "freeze" or "stop" when you see the problem and the players will do just that. (Make sure that you explain what you're doing and how they should respond before you start the game.) After you tweak the players back to what you want to address you'll have a three dimensional picture of the problem that you can show as well as talk about. Step in, make you're comments and then let them proceed. They can restart the game from that point with a first pass free or a player's choice. Don't take too long or begin a lecture, keep it under a minute. Explanations should be brief and to the point. Point out the on/off, yes/no or technical options and get the game going. Don't overuse this technique. Two or three freezes in fifteen minutes is more then enough.

- Coach an individual or the group. When you want to make a point to the team you can stop the activity and make sure that everyone hears what you have to say. Or, you can address only those that you need to during a normal stoppage and let the others carry on in the game. (You can pull someone aside while the game goes on.) The advantage to the former is that everyone hears the same thing. The advantage with the later is that you make your point to those that really need to know. The disadvantage with the former is that there are likely to be individuals that aren't involved or interested in what you're saying and they'll simply tune you out. "Why are we stopping? It's not my problem" or "Oh no, him again!"

- Coach the opposition. If you want the players to work on a particular problem but the opposition isn't cooperating, spend some time coaching them. For example, you want the attackers in a game of 5v2 to move the ball quickly but the two defenders aren't working together so the attackers don't have to work very hard. You can coach the two defenders on how to work better together then, when they are putting enough pressure on the attackers, you can get back to the lesson as planned.

- Stand where you can see the group you're working with. Avoid standing in the center of an activity, instead stand where you can see across everyone and have a clear perspective of what's going on. An exception to this is when you're shadowing a particular player for a few minutes during a game. You may want to stay close by them to coach them in the game.

- Play as a neutral player. This allows you to have a direct impact on the game and the players. You can slow down or speed up the game, as you like. You can also talk with players like a player and this works well if you want to coach an individual. You use "player speak" not a "coaches voice." Instruction tends to be short, direct and to the point. "Play simple" "Next time earlier" are common comments on the field. However, if you are not equal to or above the level of the players stay off of the field. You really don't want to be a problem yourself.

- Coach the players in the game and not something out of a book. Coaches are tempted to try something they have seen even if it has nothing to do with the problems the players actually have. This goes back to diagnosing the problems and settling on the biggest one first. Helping them to play better soccer is more important then learning how to run an overlap.

- During games don't be a ball watcher. Too often coaches only see what is going on in the immediate area around the ball. When was the last time you checked your goalkeeper's position during your own corner kicks?

- Watch for the hidden moments in the match. The new parent coach can become fixated on the static moments in the game. Throw-ins, goal kicks, kick offs, almost any moment that involves a restart of the game. These moments are easy to see, everyone has a place to be, a job to do and they can be seen in place. It's like studying a movie still as opposed to the film. Look for the dynamic "moments" in the game and you'll begin to see that, more often then not, things go wrong because a player was "A little too early or a little too late."

- Keep team time for the team. With the majority of youth teams only practicing between two to three hours a week, plus a one-hour game, try to avoid spending time on things that the kids can do by themselves, with a parent or a friend. Things like juggling, throw-ins and practicing step over moves against imaginary opponents are a drain on the team time. There's a reason why the kids don't practice these things at home and it's usually because it's boring and they're not interested.

- With that being said, go ahead and assign homework. Challenge them with "Beat your own record" activities. When they're not involved in a game at practice, during an active rest, they can have little challenges with a partner. How many juggles can you do today? Can they lift the ball three times in a row off of the ground? Can they complete a circuit? The ones who get involved voluntarily are showing you their level of commitment, e.g. motivation.

- Use open and closed ended questions together. Open-ended questions allow the players to express themselves while closed ended questions require a yes/no response or a very short, simple answer. For example, "What went wrong?" is open-ended. Their answer gives you better understanding to what they were seeing and thinking. "Which pass is better, A or B?" is close ended and allows you to move them in the direction that you want. You'll have to use both types in order to understand the problems and help the players with the solutions.

- If you have one hour to practice you really only have 45 minutes. With players arriving late, leaving early, rest breaks setting up different fields and the like the amount of time that you actually have is never what the field permit says. You have to take that into account in planning the session. Don't plan so much that you get nothing done. Have a warm-up game, something that you can feed the players into. 2v2's, four square and the like. A smaller version of your main game or even an opposite theme is next. For example, if you want to concentrate on the team coming out in the Big Goal, Two Small Goals game, focusing on their support and passing, play some 5v2. Or, since you already plan on working on passing and support play balance it out with a 1v2 No Teams Game. That way the players will be able to get some work in on their individual attacking play and defending.

- If your warm up game is flowing well, let it run. Say you have a 2v2 Passing Game mini-tournament going as the warm up and the kids are really into it. Skip the second, even third item in your plan. If the kids are really engaged in a worthwhile activity, and you stop it, there's no guarantee that they'll bring that same level of commitment to the next game. You might be trading a "Winner take all" high speed game for a "Not this again" uphill slog. It's a coaching decision.

- On the other hand what do you do if they have the talent for a game but just can't or don't get it? You can pull the plug and move on, or, you can stay with the game until they get it right. Sometimes players intentionally or unintentionally sabotage the plan. Either through lack of concentration or lack of effort. They go through the motions in order to get to the next activity, often the scrimmage. This maybe a time to teach some discipline or perseverance. You can elect to stick with it until they get it right. Sometimes the later has to become the lesson in place of the immediate technical tactical objective. It's another coaching decision.

Conclusion

Small-sided games are often seen as being something the kids can look forward too at the end of practice, as a reward after they've done their work. Hopefully I've been able to demonstrate that they are much more the icing on the cake. In many cases they can be the entire meal.

If you have been using the Physical Education model up to now you might find that letting go is hard. Using small-sided games requires patience and confidence that the kids really can learn from the games. The overt, coach centered, style of instruction is replaced by a covert, guided discovery approach.

The Physical Education model is centered on teaching. It assumes that the children are empty vessels waiting to be filled and that information must be poured in before any progress can be made. This leads to the lines, lectures and drills that are so prominent on today's training fields. When this methodology is combined with the well meaning but inexperienced parent coach you can appreciate how slowly development takes place, if it takes place at all. Soccer gets lost in the organization of the lesson plan. Barbara Knapp sums up the problem when she asks, "When does the teaching stop, and the learning start?" Using the Physical Education model you have to wonder when this moment takes place.

Using the small-sided games model allows children to learn the game in a holistic context. They learn the game through games. It also takes into account that you cannot teach faster then they can learn. It's not a question of how much, or how fast you can put "knowledge" in each child, rather it's how much you can draw out. Each child learns and contributes at their own pace, for their own reasons and on their schedule.

The soccer education process isn't so much about mastering a set of techniques and skills. That approach takes you right back to the lines and lectures. It's more about solving problems. In his book, Brilliant Orange, David Winner captures this idea when he observes that "Opponents were not seen as foes to be fought and beaten; rather as posing a problem which had to be solved." Using small-sided games is the most efficient and effective way to create meaningful, realistic problems for the kids to solve. The solution, as long as it's within the rules, belongs to the players.

Appendix

Soccer Problem Worksheet				
What moment is in question?	*Own team in possession.*	*Opponents in possession.*	*Change of possession, winning possession.*	*Change of possession, losing possession.*
What is the problem?	*What are we doing/not doing?*		*What are the opponents doing /not doing?*	
Who is responsible?	*Who has to deal with this problem?*			
Where does the problem take place?	*Attacking third.*	*Middle third.*	*Defensive third.* *The left side.*	
When does the problem occur?	*What event triggers the problem?*			
Why does the problem happen?	*Where is the breakdown in TIC?*			

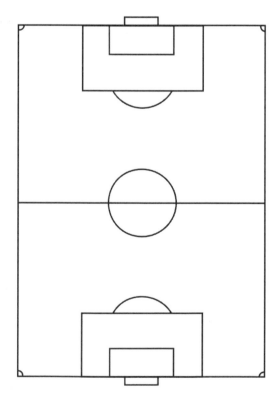
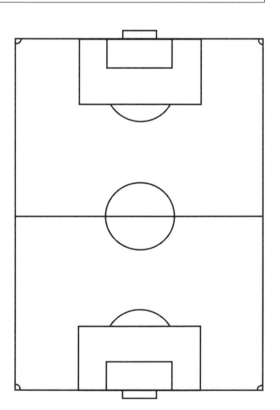

Appendix A

Training for:				Location:		Date:
Analysis of problem:						
Objectives for the session:						
Main moment:				Field third:	No. Of players:	
Basic organization:		Action/rules/progressions:			Coaching points:	

Appendix B

Player Evaluation – Name:	Date:
Contact:	**Identification:**

3 = Good   2 = Average   1 = Below Average

1.	**Speed of play.**
	a. Mental speed. 3 2 1
	b. Physical speed. 3 2 1
2.	**Technique.**
	a. Do they have the skills necessary to fill the role at the required level? 3 2 1
	b. 1v1 in possession. 3 2 1
	c. 1v1 opponents in possession. 3 2 1
3.	**Contribution to the game.**
	a. Own team in possession. 3 2 1
	b. Opponents in possession. 3 2 1
	c. Transition, winning/losing possession. 3 2 1
4.	**Personality/mentality.**
	a. Alert/concentration. 3 2 1
	b. Composure. 3 2 1
	c. Courage. 3 2 1
	d. Leadership. 3 2 1
	e. Competitiveness. 3 2 1
	f. Human relations, teammates, opponents, referee, coach. 3 2 1
5.	**Insight.**
	a. Do they grasp things quickly? 3 2 1
	b. Can they read, anticipate situations? 3 2 1
6.	**Body orientation. Dominate nature.**
	a. Both feet. 3 2 1
	b. Left foot. 3 2 1
	c. In the air. 3 2 1
	d. Right foot. 3 2 1
7.	**Role in the team/game.**
	a. Goal scorer.
	b. Goal maker.
	c. Ball winner.
	d. Goalkeeper.
	e. Center, left, right, ahead of the ball, behind the ball.
8.	**Notes:**

Appendix C

Team-Match Evaluation Guide

Analysis of: _____ Date:_____

Opponent:_____

Venue:_____ K.O._____

Weather:_____

Conditions:_____

Match:_____

Score at half:_____ Final:_____

1) Basic organization of the team:

a) In possession:_____

_____

b) Not in possession:_____

_____

c)In transition:_____

_____

_____

2) Basic organization of the lines:

a) Top players:_____

_____

_____

b) Midfield:_____

_____

_____

c)Backs:_____

_____

_____

d) Goalkeeper:_____

_____

3) Key Players:_____

_____

_____

_____

4) Cooperation between the lines:_____

_____

_____

_____

_____

Appendix D

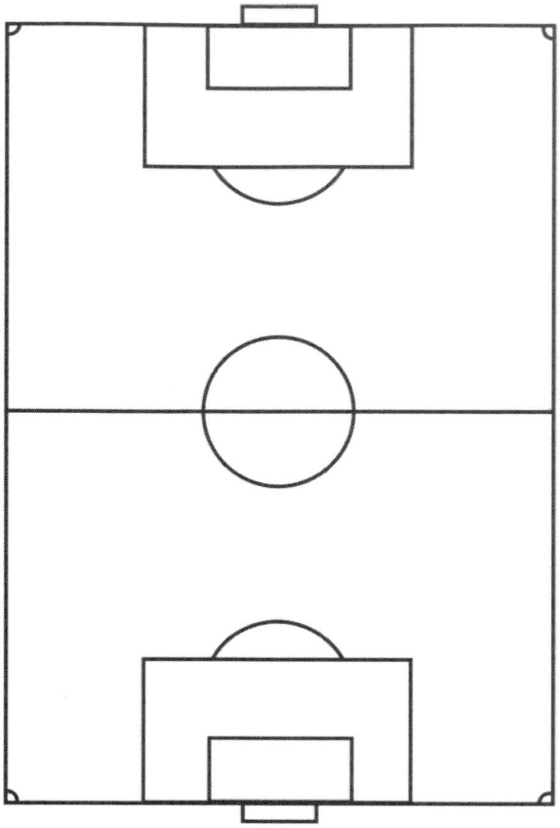

5) Use and affect of substitutes:_____
_____
_____
_____

6) Change at half:_____
_____
_____
_____

7) Method of build up-attack:_____
_____
_____
_____

8) Method of defense:_____
_____
_____
_____

9) Execution of restart plays:_____
_____
_____
_____

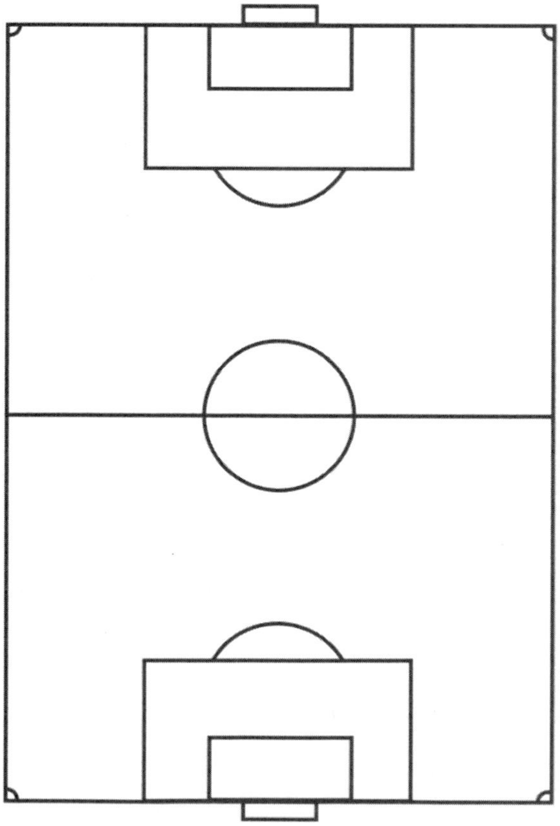

10) How are goals created:_____
_____
_____
_____

11) General description of:
a) First half:_____
_____
_____
_____

b) Second half:_____
_____
_____
_____

Appendix E

Match/Player Control Sheet:

Date:_____ **Match:**_____

Name	1st	2nd	3rd	4th

Name	1st	2nd	3rd	4th

Appendix F

4v4 Tournament Schedule		Game I		Game II			Game III			Game IV			Game V		Total Pts.	Finish
#	Name	Team.	Pts.	Team.	Pts.	Cum.	Team.	Pts.	Cum.	Team.	Pts.	Cum.	Team.	Pts.		
1																
2																
3																
4																
5																
6																
7																
8																
9																
10																
11																
12																
13																
14																
15																
16																

Appendix G

Tournament and Festival Score Sheet

Win = 10 points / Draw = 5 points / loss = 0 / Each goal = 1 point

Teams	Score	Game 1	Points	
A v B	-		A -	B -
C v D	-		C -	D -
E v F	-		E -	F -
G v H	-		G -	H -
I v J	-		I -	J -

		Game 2		
A v B	-		A -	B -
C v D	-		C -	D -
E v F	-		E -	F -
G v H	-		G -	H -
I v J	-		I -	J -

		Game 3		
A v B	-		A -	B -
C v D	-		C -	D -
E v F	-		E -	F -
G v H	-		G -	H -
I v J	-		I -	J -

		Game 4		
A v B	-		A -	B -
C v D	-		C -	D -
E v F	-		E -	F -
G v H	-		G -	H -
I v J	-		I -	J -

		Game 5		
A v B	-		A -	B -
C v D	-		C -	D -
E v F	-		E -	F -
G v H	-		G -	H -
I v J	-		I -	J -

Appendix H

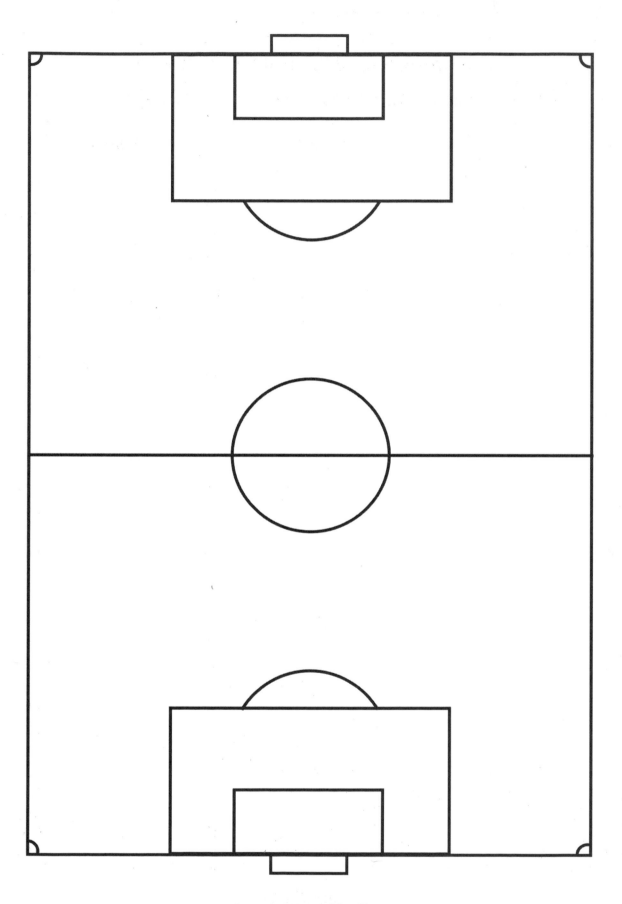

Appendix I